BADLY

BEHAVED

WOMEN

Published in 2022 by Welbeck
An imprint of Welbeck Non-Fiction Limited,
part of Welbeck Publishing Group.

Based in London and Sydney
www.welbeckpublishing.com

A catalogue record for this book is available from the British Library.

ISBN: 978 1 80279 236 2

10 9 8 7 6 5 4 3 2 1

Printed in Dubai

Editorial: Isabel Wilkinson
Design: Katie Baxendale, Luana Gobbo
Picture Manager: Steve Behan
Production: Marion Storz

MIX
Paper | Supporting
responsible forestry
FSC
www.fsc.org FSC® C004800

BADLY BEHAVED WOMEN

THE STORY OF MODERN FEMINISM

ANNA-MARIE CROWHURST

WELBECK

CONTENTS

INTRODUCTION

O ver 170 years ago, women started a protest that began a powerful global movement. The history of the women's liberation movement in the twentieth and twenty-first centuries is a story that underpins and reflects modern culture as we know it. Feminism has grown from a niche organization that fought for female education, and then the vote, to a global movement demanding true equality for all and a tearing down of the structures of the world that have repressed half the population for thousands of years.

From the vote to the pill, workplace equality to reproductive rights and intersectionality to representation, the women of each decade have tackled their own set of issues, resulting in some seismic leaps (and some baby steps) forward. Some truly enormous historical moments in women's politics – the Ford Dagenham strike, *Roe v. Wade*, Greenham Common, the Women's March, #MeToo – have acted as agents of change, and some powerful women's leaders have emerged, from Betty Friedan, Gloria Steinem and Angela Davis to Hillary Clinton, Chimamanda Ngozi Adichie and Michelle Obama, each one of them representative of the things women can achieve when they are given the tools to do so.

Opposite: British suffragettes wear symbolic white at the 1913 funeral procession of Emily Wilding Davison, who died after being trampled protesting women's right to vote at the Derby.

Previous pages: Pussy Riot stages an anti-Putin protest in Moscow's Red Square, 2012. Members were arrested and detained. One month later they were sentenced to two years in prison following a conviction for "hooliganism".

It is impossible to look at how far women have come and not feel that the twenty-first century is the best yet in which to be a woman. Writing this, I look around me and see feminism everywhere. I see active protest, now reclaimed by a new generation, who are politicized, powerful and unafraid to stand up for what is right. I see Greta Thunberg continuing to campaign for climate justice on the world stage. I see Jacinda Ardern making headlines with her decisive – and ultimately, effective leadership around Covid precautions. I see a historic number of women across the US Senate and Congress and in the Spanish Parliament. In 2021, Sweden elected its first female Prime Minister, Magdalena Andersson. And in 2020 Kamala Harris made history when she was elected Vice President of the United States, becoming the first woman, the first black American, and the first South Asian American to hold the post. I see diverse representations of bodies and genders and races in advertising and on screen (but not enough. Not yet).

The writing of this book has been an edifying and enlightening experience. There is not enough space to include every story or aspect of the movement I passionately longed to and I apologize for these limitations imposed by space. Some of the stories I encountered moved me to tears – the personal sacrifices made by the suffragettes who starved themselves to enfranchise women. The women around the world who have risked everything to campaign for access to abortion and contraception. The fact that Judy Chicago's *Dinner Party* was mobbed when it opened in 1979, the year I was born. I have felt inspired by the women who lifted up their voices and made things happen, such as the women of Pussy Riot, who sacrificed their freedom to highlight oppression. And Malala Yousafzai, who fought to be educated and, in doing so, changed the world.

Forms of mass protest have always supported and empowered women to fight for their right to equality. I salute the women of the

2010s who made their voices heard when they said #MeToo and #TimesUp. And the millions of women around the world who came together in street protests to speak truth to power on the Women's March – I was there myself, in London, and could feel, as I walked shoulder to shoulder with other women who sang, shouted and cheered that this was a turning point in our history.

I would like to dedicate this book to each and every person who has stood up for women in a small way, or a big one, and tried to move things forward. I hope this book will serve as a testament to the progress made and an indication of what we can do, when we come together.

A note on definitions in the text – I have used the words "women" and "trans women" to differentiate between cisgender women and those who identify as trans women. In some instances, "women" in the collective may unknowingly refer to those who identify differently, and for that I can only apologize for any unintentional offence caused.

Anna-Marie Crowhurst, 2022

1900–
1970

DEEDS
NOT WORDS
PROTESTS IN PETTICOATS

The women who won the vote have gone down in history for their sacrifice and valour in the face of arrest, imprisonment and force-feeding. At the heart of the suffragettes' campaign was a commitment to direct action, no matter what the cost.

For as long as women have been advocating for their rights, they have used direct action as protest. The demos of the 1960s, the flour bombs of the 1970s and the marches of the 2010s all have their roots in the actions of the earliest feminist campaigners: the brave women we know as the suffragettes. By the 1860s the women's suffrage movement was gaining momentum in Britain. Suffragists argued for women's enfranchisement in the form of voting reform. Their societies lobbied politicians for the vote, held public meetings, wrote newspaper articles and organized petitions. The movement began to coalesce in 1897, when 17 societies combined as the National Union of Women's Suffrage Societies (NUWSS), led by Millicent Fawcett, and published pamphlets on domestic topics such as working conditions, education and children. So far, so polite.

As the century turned with little progress, frustration with the limitations of the "Votes for Women" campaign set in. In 1903 the Women's Social and Political Union (WSPU) was founded by Emmeline Pankhurst and her daughters. Themselves committed

Opposite: Banner, made c.1908 by the Wimbledon branch of the WSPU.

DEEDS NOT WORDS

WIMBLEDON

W.S P U

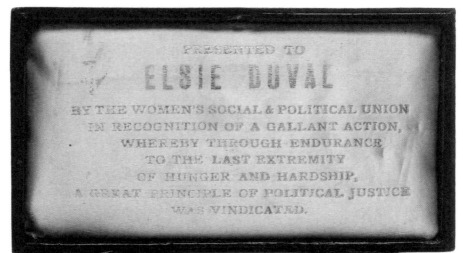

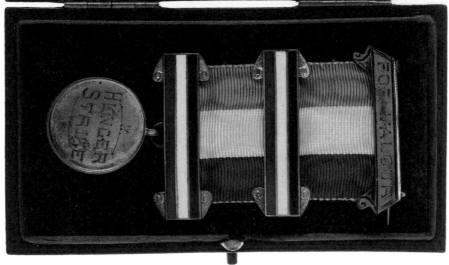

Above: Medal awarded to suffragette Elsie Duval for bravery while on hunger strike in prison in 1912. She was force-fed nine times.

What a Woman may be, and yet not have the Vote

MAYOR   NURSE   MOTHER   DOCTOR or TEACHER   FACTORY HAND

What a Man may have been, & yet not lose the Vote

CONVICT   LUNATIC   Proprietor of white Slaves   Unfit for Service   DRUNKARD

suffrage campaigners, the Pankhursts had come to believe that where polite petitions and pamphlets had failed, drawing public attention to their cause would succeed. In 1905 they came up with a bold new motto to reflect their aims, "Deeds Not Words", with attention-grabbing branding for banners and sashes using symbolic colours of white (for purity), green (for hope) and purple (for loyalty and dignity). By now suffrage societies were forming across Europe, as well as the International Women's Suffrage Alliance, which united suffrage chapters from all over the world. The USA and Britain, however, seemed to enjoy the most radical forms of protesting.

In the USA, too, women were mobilized into action. Alice Paul – inspired by a visit to Britain during which she participated in WSPU

Above: Designed by London's Suffrage Atelier collective, this 1913 poster shows the double standards around voting rights.

protests – formed the National Women's Party (NWP), organizing parades and pickets and lobbying Congress for voting reform. In 1913 she led 8,000 women from the Capitol to the White House. In 1917 the NWP began 18 months of White House picketing, holding up signs that read, "Mr. President, how long must women wait for liberty?" Paul was imprisoned and began a hunger strike. The amendment granting US women the right to vote was finally passed by Congress on June 4, 1919 and was ratified on August 18, 1920.

In London, the WSPU organized large-scale protests outside Parliament and street marches, then swiftly began a militant campaign with headline-grabbing tactics. Women smashed shop windows with bricks, cut telegraph wires, set fire to pillar boxes and buildings, and chained themselves to the railings of Downing Street. A nationwide bombing and arson campaign was designed to provoke maximum attention. By 1909 WSPU members were setting on Winston Churchill with a horsewhip and even vandalizing Prime Minister Herbert Asquith's car. By the 1910s they were defacing artworks and displays in galleries, and the newspaper front pages were regularly splashed with dramatic images of these protests, iconic images of defiance we recognize today: the women in their trimmed bonnets and white dresses defiantly holding placards; women being dragged away by policemen; the unmoving form of Emily Wilding Davison on the racetrack at Epsom. By now the street protests had become violent clashes between police and suffragettes, with women physically assaulted and arrested. Those who were arrested and imprisoned began starvation campaigns, and were force-fed with tubes.

Opposite: Advert for the WSPU newspaper *The Suffragette* designed by Hilda Dallas, c.1914. Joan of Arc was the suffragettes' patron saint and reflected their increasingly violent tactics.

Overleaf: Members of the American National Women's Party, known as the "Silent Sentinels", protest outside the White House, 1917. President Wilson did not support women's suffrage.

THE
SUFFRAGETTE
W.S.P.U.
JUSTICE
EDITED BY
CHRISTABEL
PANKHURST.
1D
WEEKLY.
H.M. Dallas.

SUFFRAGE AROUND THE WORLD

The early part of the twentieth century saw women across the world rising up to demand their voting rights. In Finland, a socialist uprising involving mass demonstrations had resulted in women's enfranchisement in 1906. Norway gave women the vote in 1913, Denmark and Iceland in 1915. Austria and Germany, as well as most of Canada, followed suit in 1918. The USA caved in 1920. Britain's Representation of the People Act 1918 gave the vote to

women over 30 who owned property, or were married to a man who did. All women over 21 (then the legal voting age for men) did not get the right to vote in Britain until 1928. Spain did not let women vote until 1931. In France it was 1944, Italy 1945. As the middle of the century approached, many women had the vote but the battle for women's rights had only just begun.

TIMELINE OF WOMEN'S SUFFRAGE

1792 Mary Wollstonecraft argues for women's suffrage in her book *A Vindication of the Rights of Woman*.

1848 Seneca Falls Convention in New York calls for women's suffrage, as well as working rights and educational opportunities.

1869 The UK Parliament grants single women taxpayers the right to vote in municipal elections. In the USA, the new Territory of Wyoming grants women the right to vote and the National Woman Suffrage Association is formed.

1893 New Zealand becomes the first country in the world to grant universal suffrage to all women.

1902 Australian women over the age of 21 are granted the vote in federal elections. South Australia and Western Australia had granted women rights to vote in 1894 and 1899 respectively. The rest of the states follow and Australian women have full voting rights by 1908. Aboriginal women (and men) are granted the right to vote in 1962.

1906 The Grand Duchy of Finland (then a part of Russia) is the first country in Europe to implement full universal suffrage, including women. Nineteen women elected to parliament the following year.

1913 Norway becomes the first independent country to grant universal suffrage to all women.

1915 Denmark grants women full voting rights; they were allowed to vote in municipal elections in 1908.

1917 Russia's Provisional government enfranchises women.

1918 Canada gives full suffrage to black and white women. Newfoundland grants suffrage in 1925 and Quebec in 1940. Asian women are granted the vote (with men) in 1948, and First Nations and Inuit women (and men) are given full voting rights in 1960.

1918   Germany and Austria get full suffrage, including women, after the breakdown of the House of Hapsburg. After Poland gains independence, women are granted the right to vote. In the UK and Ireland, women aged 30 or over receive complete enfranchisement, shortly after women are allowed to sit in the House of Commons. In Czechoslovakia, the Declaration of Independence of the Czechoslovak Nation guarantees equal voting rights for men and women.

1918   Countess Constance Markievicz becomes the first woman to be elected to the UK House of Commons. She does not take her seat.

1919   In the Netherlands women's right to vote is approved and takes effect in 1920.

1920   August 26 marks the passing of the Nineteenth Amendment to the Constitution of the United States.

1921   In Sweden, all women are given the right to vote.

1922   The newly independent Irish Free State gives women the equal right to vote from the age of 21. In Hungary, women vote for the first time, despite plans to introduce suffrage going back to 1818.

1928   The United Kingdom lowers the voting age for women to 21.

1929   Ecuador grants women limited voting rights, the second independent country in South America to do so after Uruguay in 1917.

1930   South Africa allows white women aged 21 and over to vote. In 1984 all mixed-race citizens are granted the vote and in 1994 voting rights are extended to all citizens regardless of race.

1931   Spanish women are granted limited voting rights. While women over 20 are allowed limited voting under Franco's regime, full voting rights are implemented only in 1977.

1931 Sri Lanka (at that time Ceylon) becomes one of the first South Asian countries to allow voting rights to women over the age of 21 without any restrictions.

1932 In Brazil, the right to vote is added to the Electoral Code and to the Brazilian constitution in 1934. Thailand also gives women the right to vote.

1934 Turkey gives women the right to vote in national elections. Cuba also extends voting rights to women.

1937 In the Philippines a referendum wins by a landslide allowing women to vote; this is the first legal right granted to women in the country.

1944 The French provisional government extends the right to vote to women. French-controlled Algeria grants Muslim women the right to vote in 1958.

1945 The provisional government of Italy grants full enfranchisement to women. Partial suffrage had been introduced by Mussolini's government in 1925.

1946 In Romania, suffrage with many restrictions had been in place since 1938, but full voting rights are granted in 1946. In Japan women's suffrage is enacted at a national level, although women had been allowed to vote in some prefectures since 1880.

1947 In Argentina, over 3 million newly enfranchised women vote in the 1947 elections. Pakistan enacts full suffrage upon independence, thanks to a movement led by the wives and female relatives of leading politicians.

1947 In India, some women had been granted voting rights in the early twentieth century, dependent on education, religion and class. The government of India enacts equal voting rights for both men and women.

1952 The United Nations Convention on the Political Rights of Women decrees that "women shall be entitled to vote in all elections on equal terms with men, without any discrimination."

1953 Mexican women gain the right to vote in 1947 for some local elections and for national elections in 1953, after a struggle dating to the nineteenth century.

1962 Algerian women are given the full right to vote after the War of Independence.

1963 In Iran, a referendum in January overwhelmingly approved by voters gives women the right to vote. Morocco also grants women voting rights.

1971 Switzerland becomes the last Western republic to grant women's suffrage. A previous referendum on suffrage had been defeated in 1959.

1971 Bangladesh reconfirms women's right to vote.

1976 From 1931, Portuguese women are allowed to vote if they have a degree; full rights are only granted in 1976.

1994–2006 The Gulf States gradually grant women the right to vote. Oman extends rights in 1994, Qatar in 1999 and Bahrain in 2001. The right to vote was given to women in Kuwait in 1985; though this was later removed, it was reinstated in 2005.

2015 Saudi Arabian women vote in and run for local and municipal elections for the first time. Women can also be appointed to the Shura council, an unelected governing body.

HELEN PANKHURST

ACTIVIST & AUTHOR

ON FEMINISM THEN AND NOW

Feminism is important to me – perhaps not surprisingly so – given that I am the great-granddaughter of Emmeline, leader of the suffragette movement. But I am also the granddaughter of Sylvia who disagreed with her mother and her older sister, Christabel, about some campaigning tactics and how to address the intersection between class and gender. I understood early on how schisms are very much part of women's history.

In the build-up to the centenary of some women getting the vote, as part of my own journey I reflected, interviewed and then in 2018 published *Deeds Not Words: The Story of Women's Rights, Then and Now.* The book has subsequently provided a tool for discussion and debate on how far we have come.

I also convened the Centenary Action Group, a coalition which aims to use the period to 2028 – the centenary of Equal Franchise – to raise awareness of the constraints around equal representation. Its tagline is #StillMarching. Also, I became involved in the GM4Women2028 coalition, which highlights women's experiences in Greater Manchester, birthplace of the suffragettes. The message: #WeCanDoBetter.

For many feminists, marching seems to be in our DNA. I have led wonderfully colourful marches and rallies on International Women's Day in London, celebrating, in March4Women, linkages between those interested in the history of feminism, current-day UK-based feminist activists and global feminists.

The international perspective has been part of my make-up because I grew up and still work in Ethiopia. My job with CARE in Ethiopia has been multi-sectoral and included strengthening the agency of young girls, addressing the social norms and the structural barriers that continue to blight the lives of women and girls.

Feminism isn't a simple add-on. It is at the core of my identity and of my work. "Fun and Purpose" is my personal motto.

WE WEAR
THE PANTS
THE STORY OF WOMEN'S SLACKS

In the 1920s, there was a fashion revolution: trousers for women.
Introduced by the zany flappers, women wearing pants
signalled something much bigger than a mere fashion trend:
it was freedom, at least of a sort.

In the summer of 2021 in Britain, trousers were in the news. Wirral Grammar School for Girls in England announced they were amending their uniform policy after a student-organized petition demanding girls should be able to wear trousers gained 13,000 signatures. One hundred years before, in 1919, in Puerto Rico, Luisa Capetillo was arrested and jailed for daring to wear trousers. Capetillo wasn't just being experimental with her fashion: as one of Puerto Rico's first suffragists, she was making a point about the expectations around women's clothing – and, by extension, women.

In the early part of the twentieth century, argument around women's clothing wasn't new. In reaction to the restrictive trends of crinolines, bustles and tight lacing, the "dress reformists" of the 1850s had argued for trousers on practical grounds. In Britain and the USA, "Bloomerism" sprang up. Entangled with the idea of early feminism was that of "freedom dress" – clothes in which women

Opposite: *Vogue* cover showing a woman wearing sporty wide-legged trousers, illustrated by Eduardo Garcia Benito, July 1930.

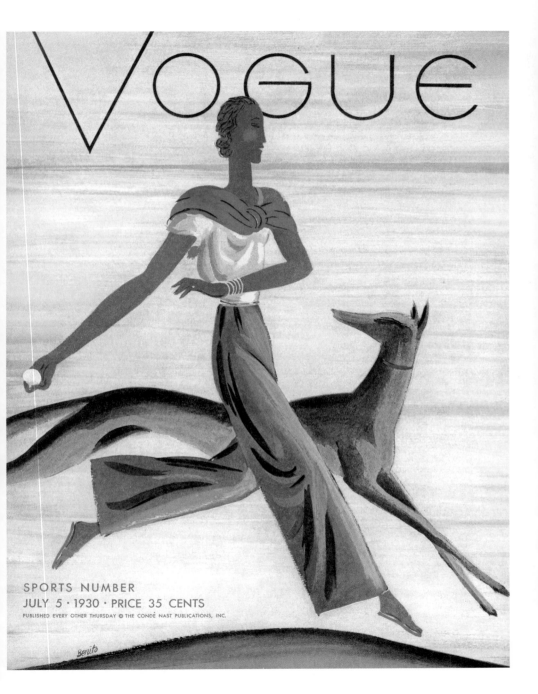

VOGUE

SPORTS NUMBER
JULY 5 · 1930 · PRICE 35 CENTS
PUBLISHED EVERY OTHER THURSDAY © THE CONDÉ NAST PUBLICATIONS, INC.

Benito

· 32 ·

could breathe, and move. A so-called "liberty bodice" and bloomers seemed a possible, decorous solution. There were rumours of women being arrested in New York City for trouser-wearing, while adverts and cartoons poked fun at the very idea of women not wearing skirts.

The 1920s saw many women in the Western world enfranchised, both to vote and to wear trousers. Set loose by the general unbuttoning in the wake of the First World War – and in North America, the post-war boom economy – the set of liberated women known as flappers emerged. The flappers scandalized their mothers by wearing make-up and shearing their hair off, by hareing around in motorcars and Charlestoning, corset-less, in nightclubs. And most importantly, they slipped into pyjama-style suits and fashionable floaty bell-bottoms, embracing the new trend for trousers.

Coco Chanel led this sartorial charge, wafting chicly around in wide-leg beach trousers. Chanel had made her name in France, creating radical pared-down designs that allowed women freedom of movement and liberation from fuss, frills and winsome pastel colours, replacing them with monochromatic designs incorporating elements of menswear and tailoring, and a relaxed silhouette. The Chanel look caught on like wildfire. For the first time in many hundreds of years, women suddenly had the physical freedom to ride bicycles and horses, play sports, turn cartwheels and generally enjoy themselves, without the need for showing their knickers and quite so much restrictive, complicated underwear to boot. Among the younger and hipper, trousers for women took off. Witness Marlene Dietrich starring in 1930's *Morocco*, swanking about in a tuxedo and top hat, her eyebrow archly raised. By the end of the 1930s, trousers were a female fashion staple.

Opposite: Early adopter of trousers Coco Chanel at her home in the French Riviera, c.1930.

Above: Doreen Bacchus of the Women's Land Army wearing standard issue breeches, at a Women's Timber Corps Training Camp in Suffolk, England, 1942. Uniforms like these helped to popularize trousers as womenswear.

Opposite: Silver screen superstar Marlene Dietrich, 1933. Dietrich was an early adopter of trousers, and had become famous for her tailored trouser suits.

While women seemed to be liberating themselves in a sartorial sense, the early part of the twentieth century saw activism around women's rights bubbling under. The smashed windows and the stunts had contributed to getting the vote, and in 1929 in the UK, the first general election in which all women could have their say saw record-breaking voter numbers. But the suffragettes had not been replaced by a comparably radical feminist movement. The flappers embodied a spirit and energy that reflected the world's post-war optimism and newness, and though they exercised their rights to vote, they were not as militant as their suffragette forebears.

Trousers were to make waves again with the advent of the Second World War. In Europe, shortages in elastic and nylon, as well as clothes rationing, meant stockings and girdles became in short supply – trouser-wearing was the simple, patriotic solution. At the same time, thousands of women joined the services and began to wear uniforms, which in the case of land girls and foresters meant practical pants. Other women were conscripted into manual war work in factories or as engineers and mechanics, and wore overalls. By the end of the war it seemed trousers had truly arrived for women, and this time for good.

Right: Worker riveting an A-20 bomber at the Douglas Aircraft Company plant in California, 1942. Trousers were essential for this type of job, and a badge of honour.

A ROOM OF ONE'S OWN
CREATIVITY VERSUS THE PATRIARCHY

The interwar period saw women able to vote but still subject to the restrictions of society's patriarchal gender roles. Female creatives discovered the struggle of making art when it competed with marriage, motherhood and domesticity.

Where art flourishes, so do radical ideas. So it was for the creative women of the early twentieth century. The prevailing artistic mood of the first few decades of the century was modernism – advocating newness, simplicity and experimentation. Modernists were vegetarians and wore avant-garde fashions; they were queer; they were anti-war and pro-free love – and, often, they were feminists.

Writers like Katherine Mansfield and Marianne Moore, and artists like Georgia O'Keeffe and Lee Miller explored the feminine condition through themes of self-image, domesticity, relationships, fertility and motherhood. This reflected the experience of the age: once married, female creatives often discovered that their seemingly liberal relationships – despite their polyamory and sexual experimentation – reverted to prescribed gender norms, with child-rearing and housework falling on women at the great cost of time to do their art.

Long before the invention of labour-saving devices and modern detergents, housework in the early twentieth century was laborious and time-consuming. The painter Vanessa Bell, while living in the

Above: Isadora Duncan dancing, 1904. Inspired by the ancient Greeks, Duncan performed with bare feet and arms, and in daring costumes. She wasn't quite so liberated in her personal life.

open-minded structures and privileged echelons of the Bloomsbury Group, still found herself distracted by cleaning. "How I hate these domestic duties..." she wrote in a letter, quoted in Virginia Nicholson's *Among the Bohemians* – "I haven't been able to paint yet." Ford Madox Ford's partner, the painter Sheila Bowen, found that after "struggling through" the day's chores and looking after her daughter she "simply had not got any creative vitality to spare".

While male artists were free to create, released from the boredom and worry of domestic tasks, women often found their creativity stymied by childbearing and motherhood, which in the age before mass contraception and decriminalized abortion, was difficult to restrict or plan. Isadora Duncan, who had three children while single, wrote of the particular physical strain of pregnancy in her autobiography, *My Life*. "My nimble feet grew slower..." she wrote. "Where was my lovely, youthful naiad form? Where my ambition? My fame ... With what a price we pay for the glory of motherhood."

Rebecca West, who wrote in her sharp, fiery prose on topics such as single motherhood, suffragism and female sexuality, said in 1913, "I myself have never been able to find out precisely what a feminist is. I only know that people call me a feminist whenever I express sentiments that differentiate me from a doormat."

The German Dada pioneer Hannah Höch made art inspired by her interest in gender roles and women who subverted them, using photomontage techniques to explore depictions of the female body. "I wish to blur the firm boundaries which we self-certain people tend to delineate around all we can achieve," she said. Of her partner, the artist Raoul Hausmann, she was to declare, "Poor Raoul. He needed constant encouragement to carry out his ideas and achieve anything at all lasting. If I hadn't devoted so much of my time to looking after him I might have achieved more myself."

Opposite: Portrait of Virginia Woolf by her sister Vanessa Bell, c.1912. Both sisters faced the struggle to be creative despite their domestic circumstances.

Above: Cover to the first edition of Virginia Woolf's *A Room of One's Own*, published by the Hogarth Press in 1929.

Opposite: Hannah Höch and Raoul Hausmann at 1920's First International Dada Fair in Berlin. To the left hangs her photomontage piece, *Cut with the Kitchen Knife Dada Through the Last Weimar Beer-Belly Cultural Epoch in Germany* (1919).

British-born Mina Loy led a peripatetic artistic existence in continental Europe and America. She painted, and wrote poems and novels that explored themes of female experience. In 1914, in her polemic *Feminist Manifesto*, she urged women to "leave off looking to men to find out what you are not – seek within yourselves to find out what you are".

Some were luckier. The poet and suffragist campaigner Edna St. Vincent Millay married Eugen Boissevain, who looked after things while she focused on writing. "I have nothing to do with my household," she said in 1931. "Eugen does all that kind of thing." She added, "I could never have married the kind of person with whom I would have had to settle down ... My husband is responsive to my every mood. That's the only way in which I can live and be what I am."

In 1929, Virginia Woolf voiced many of her contemporaries' frustrations around societal constructs that limited women's education and artistic creation, and the intangible inequalities that enfranchising women had not solved, when she published *A Room of One's Own*. "Women have sat indoors all these millions of years," she wrote, "so that by this time the very walls are permeated by their creative force, which has, indeed, so overcharged the capacity of bricks and mortar that it must needs harness itself to pens and brushes and business and politics." To write fiction, she said, a woman needed money and "a room of her own". But for many women those two things were far out of reach – and would be for decades to come.

Opposite: Edna St. Vincent Millay, 1941. The poet was supported by a husband who was happy to oversee all things domestic.

EMELI SANDÉ

SINGER & SONGWRITER

ON THE NEED FOR A STUDIO
OF ONE'S OWN

Prior to reading Virginia Woolf's *A Room of One's Own* aged 21, my primary concern had been the discrimination I faced due to my skin colour. Yet it opened my eyes to the additional challenges that lay ahead of me in regards to my gender. Woolf ignited a ferocious fire within me. I got my first tattoo, the words *"un cuarto proprio"* ("a room of one's own" in Spanish), on my left arm: a reminder of my mission.

I never questioned or thought I could change the blatant male dominance in the music industry. In the first few years of my career, I blended in as one of the guys. I drank like them, smoked like them – I was a respected member of the gang. But I still found that most writing and recording sessions involved a confusing, emotional experience that my male peers were not subjected to.

The need to prove and insist on my right to write became exhausting. The struggle to be considered as an artist and not only as a writer was never-ending. Being reduced to begging for my music not to be sent to other women they deemed prettier or more marketable was a weekly humiliation that caused me a great amount of distress. The importance of my appearance in regards to the opportunities and respect I received was shockingly apparent. No matter how I improved, or how much success I accomplished, the fight for respect seemed never-ending. I began to doubt the way I looked, my talent, and my worthiness to have autonomy over my own music. I would often question whether I was supposed to be an artist at all.

When you step into someone else's (usually a man's) studio, you are completely at their mercy. Many men I have worked with have been inviting, welcoming and respectful. However, my experiences with the men that weren't have left very deep scars. They took the joy of creating away from me, belittled me and made me feel utterly powerless.

After years of these frustrations, the need for a room of my own became unbearable. I decided to build my own studio in my home. Now I have a sacred space in which I can make mistakes without scrutiny and in which I can explore. A space I feel beautiful enough to enter and am always respected within. I invite in only those I trust. It is a beautiful sanctuary, a creative home that anchors me and nourishes my musical expression.

Today I look down at my tattoo and know more than ever that Virginia Woolf was right.

THIS WOMEN'S WORK
HOW THE WAR CHANGED EVERYTHING

When men went to war, they also created space for women, who took up vacated university places and jobs, and were empowered through war work and conscription, opening their eyes to a whole new world of possibilities.

Ten years after Virginia Woolf decried "the doors that have been shut upon women", a window was opening in many female lives. The Second World War decimated Europe – but it changed the landscape of women's lives. Women became useful, powerful and active. Women went to work.

This seismic shift occurred simply because when men went to fight, women were required to take their place. University places became available and women more acceptable to fill them. Those women who had already entered the professions began to find they had more opportunities when it came to securing posts and being promoted. In Britain in 1941 some groups of women were conscripted, and 80 per cent of married women and 90 per cent of single women immediately entered the workforce, joining the Auxiliary Territorial Service, the Women's Auxiliary Air Force and the Women's Royal Naval Service. Women suddenly drove ambulances and worked in government offices, or were land girls, nurses, codebreakers, cooks,

Opposite: 1943 work-incentive poster designed by J. Howard Miller for the War Production Board. Though only displayed briefly at the time, the image of "Rosie the Riveter" has become an enduring image of women's war work.

We Can Do It!
POST FEB. 15 TO FEB. 28
WAR PRODUCTION CO-ORDINATING COMMITTEE

spies and shipyard workers. By 1943 7.5 million women in Britain were working, with those in the women's services making up nearly half a million of them. In the USA, 3 million jobs for women were created by men going to war, with over 7 million US women working in military production as factory workers, and as streetcar attendants, welders and engineers.

In strongly anti-feminist Nazi Germany, women had been marginalized. The early 1930s had seen the education system transformed to discourage women from study, and in 1936 women were officially banned from being judges, doctors, academics and politicians. Then the war broke out. Germany reluctantly mobilized its women, who served in clerical roles at first, but as the war raged they were enlisted as aircraft defence gun operators and signal auxiliaries.

Women in France, too, were conscripted to replace men in their jobs and in armaments factories, and after occupation,

Left: Eighteen-year-old fighter Simone Segouin with fellow members of the Resistance during the liberation of Paris, 1944. Paris was occupied from 1942 to 1944 by the Nazis, with many brave women risking their lives to resist them. Segouin was awarded the Croix de Guerre.

some found domestic and clerical roles with the German forces. The Vichy government branded women as frivolous and corrupt, laying France's defeat at the feet of morally void females. Freedom for French women was curtailed – they were banned from wearing trousers, urged to embrace motherhood and domestic duties, and could no longer have a job or bank account without express permission from a husband or father.

Rejecting the regime, many women joined the Resistance – young French men in occupied France attracted attention, while women didn't, and so were absolutely essential to the movement. Legendary fighters such as Yvette Farnoux risked their lives to hand out subversive leaflets, work as couriers or send messages. Farnoux started out with small acts of resistance, such as misdirecting Nazi troops or walking down the Champs-Élysees wearing patriotic colours. She ended the war as a leader of major Resistance group MUR, and survived internment in Auschwitz and Ravensbrück.

Across the world the notion of femininity seemed to be changing. Radical imagery, like Canada's "Ronnie the Bren Gun Girl" in 1941 and Norman Rockwell's 1943 depiction of peppy "Rosie the Riveter", blazed into the public imagination. Modern women knocked in rivets, held hammers as well as babies – and discovered working was a welcome escape from the dreary monotony of childcare, housework and ration books, boosting their morale as well as their self-worth.

As women's roles were changing, so too was the culture. Now women worked and were in the services, they went out and had money to spend. In unoccupied countries rules around sexual freedom, too, were bending – the old mores seemed less important when love was fleeting and young lives were short. Soldiers came home to Britain on leave and wanted a sweetheart to take to a dance; women wanted

Opposite: Women "chippers" of shipbuilding company Marinship Corp, Sausalito, California in 1942. Their job was to remove excess metal from welded seams, previously seen as a role that was suitable only for men.

to forget rations and shiftwork in the arms of handsome men in uniform; all found that a snog or a knee-trembler during the blackout did much to banish the misery and deprivation of war. Between 1939 and 1945 more women than ever recorded were having pre-marital sex and extramarital affairs. They were contracting STDs and using contraceptives. For the first time they were more likely to know the facts of life. Hasty marriages followed prolonged absences, or the prospect of them. As women were having sex outside of marriage, so children were being born to unwed mothers and as the result of extramarital affairs while couples were separated for months and years at a time. The previous structures of the nuclear family were being blitzed along with the buildings of Britain's cities. Women no longer needed to be either virgins or mothers. They were forging a new identity.

When Simone de Beauvoir's *The Second Sex* was published in 1949, it voiced the mood of reflection that was rising all over Europe around the role of women. In a meditation on the nature of femininity itself, de Beauvoir explored the meaning of female gender identity, taking in history, religion, philosophy and laws that had objectified women since time began. And as the 1950s dawned, it seemed certain that the world would never be the same again, as far as women were concerned. In a sense that was true.

Opposite: America's 6888th Central Postal Directory Battalion march in a parade in Rouen, France 1945. The 6888th was the first and only all-black, all-female army unit to have been deployed overseas during the Second World War.

BEAUTIFUL BOREDOM
ESCAPE FROM THE KITCHEN

The 1960s saw a seismic shift for women that kick-started the inception of the women's movement. What became known as the second wave began here. And it was all because of one woman's book.

No fictional character has embodied the landscape of feminism in the early 1960s quite so well as *Mad Men*'s Betty Draper. While her husband enjoys amped-up pitch meetings, daytime drinking and pointy-busted secretaries on buzzy Madison Avenue, January Jones's Betty drifts unhappily around her perfect suburban formica prison, encased in a hard shell of corsetry and hairspray – a Hitchcock blonde in an apron, wreathed in cigarette smoke and Coty perfume. With two young children, and nothing to do beside housework, cooking and gossiping with other housewives, she is suffering from a deep sort of ennui and unhappiness that causes her hands to shake.

Betty Friedan's *The Feminine Mystique*, published in 1963, explained exactly what Betty Draper was suffering from: it was "the problem that has no name"; the "secret" that a life devoted to the traditional middle-class female ideal – of housewifery, wifedom and motherhood – did not make all women happy.

Opposite: Bored, frustrated and depressed: the *Mad Men* character Betty Draper played by January Jones, embodies Friedan's 1960s housewife.

Above: *The Feminine Mystique* (1963). The term was coined by Friedan to describe the fact that women of the period were expected to be fulfilled by marriage, housework and childcare – but surprisingly, were not.

Women had been liberated by the Second World War but their freedom was temporary. In Britain, a year after VE Day, the number of women in the workplace had dropped to around a quarter of the wartime high, as men took back their jobs and their importance. In the USA, the Cold War seemed to have created the nuclear family as an expression of Western consumerist utopia. In France, de Gaulle allowed women the vote in 1945, but the responsibility and heroism they had embraced during the war evaporated as their men returned home, eager to retake their place as head of the family. In the bombed-out cities of Germany and Austria, Trümmerfrauen (rubble women) cleared and reconstructed destroyed buildings, by order of the Allies. Living in post-war poverty with their men returning defeated and weakened, many toiled both in the home and out of it, attempting to rebuild a semblance of normality.

The 1950s saw young men becoming angry, and women returning to a subservient role, grappling with the demands of hearth and home. Women were still working, but for many this meant an agreeable job – nurse, teacher, typist perhaps – while they waited to meet Mr Right. Some went to university but society's perceived goal of this was marriage – the so-called "MRS" degree.

By 1957, 33 per cent of married British women were working, but "domestic goddess" was still the ideal. In America this structure was portrayed as a dream: the American Dream. There were now household products and labour-saving appliances that seemed to come straight out of the space age, too. Convenience foods appeared, so that the newly coined "latchkey children" could feast on Fray Bentos, fish sticks, Smash and Angel Delight, Campbell's soup and Jell-O. The fashions changed to express this new, exaggerated kind of femininity. In the 1950s, Dior's "New Look" demanded vertiginous stilettos, waspy waists and enormous skirts, recalling the restrictive crinolines of the 1860s. The early 1960s still clung to this full-skirted ideal. For feminism at least, things seemed to be slowly rolling backward.

But then came Betty Friedan. Inspired by her own sense of deep frustration, she surveyed hundreds of American women on topics such as home life, identity, children and interests. Friedan discovered that 1960s women were marrying younger than in previous decades, were dropping out of the workplace and further education (as Friedan herself had done), and were having more children. Trapped by the role that had been forced on them in this post-war utopia, they felt helpless, childlike, miserable, unfulfilled – sexually as well as spiritually – and massively depressed.

The ideas promoted in the media of the time of fulfilled housewives and evil careerist women, Friedan argued, did not only fail to reflect reality, but were mostly created by those who made laws, who ran companies manufacturing household products, who created the advertising campaigns that sold them and the magazines they appeared in – men. Friedan's book acted as a sort of collective wake-up call to this reality. These were radical ideas to some – but not to the million-plus women who bought Friedan's book, and made it one of the seminal books of the twentieth century, sparking a seismic shift in the culture that many believe started the second wave of feminism. Friedan's book had its limitations – the burgeoning civil rights movement as well as the concerns of working-class women were overlooked – but her book did something good. And what's more, the 1970s were coming.

Opposite: This 1960s UK magazine advert for Hornes of London trousers demonstrates the harmful gender stereotyping that was deemed acceptable – even funny – at the time.

Memo to masterful men...

Wearing the trousers? Then you need the best — in
Woolmark pure new wool, styled and cut by Hornes
(who else?). Stun her — gently of course — with these
slender-line whipcords from Hornes exclusive Cavalry
Line range. Note the slash-cut
pockets — just right for striking an
attitude. Strictly for men, at £6/15/-.
Long term policy: Spread the
masterful look through your ward-
robe with a Hornes Extended
Account.

Certification Trade Mark applied for
**PURE NEW
wool**

HORNES
THE ALL-ROUND STORES FOR MEN

All over London and in Principal Cities

TWO LEADING WOMEN OF 1960S FEMINISM

Florynce Kennedy

Lawyer, civil rights and women's rights advocate, Kennedy graduated from
Columbia University in 1949, then applied to Columbia Law School and was
turned down – until she threatened to sue. When she graduated in 1951 she
became one of the first black women to do so. She set up her law practice
in 1953, but the 1960s saw her become a full-time activist. In 1966, Kennedy
established the Media Workshop with the aim of combating the blatant
racism in the media and advertising of the time. She led pickets outside
advertising agencies, followed by other high-profile protests with members
of the National Organization for Women, recognizable for her trademark
cowboy hats and pink sunglasses. She demonstrated for abortion rights,
represented the Black Panthers and was a founding member of the National
Women's Political Caucus. She was one of the instigators of the Miss America
Pageant protest in 1968 and in the 1970s joined Gloria Steinem on the
lecture circuit, bringing intersectional feminism to the masses.

Gloria Steinem

The woman who became known as the world's most famous feminist and was called "the mini-skirted pinup girl of the intelligentsia" by the *Washington Post*, Steinem started out as a journalist in New York City covering topics like the pill for *Esquire* and abortion speakouts for *New York* magazine. In 1969 Steinem was publishing persuasive, sparky essays on gender equality, such as 1969's "After Black Power, Women's Liberation" in *New York* magazine. She campaigned for the Equal Rights Amendment, spoke out at an event to legalize abortion, and kick-started a high-profile career. Approachable and with a talent for getting her message out accessibly, Steinem spent the 1970s speaking on feminist themes at protests, demos and on television, as well as taking part in activism. In 1971 Steinem founded *Ms.* magazine with Dorothy Pitman Hughes. She went on to help fund many feminist lobby groups, including the National Women's Political Caucus and the Women's Action Alliance.

CALL HERSELF FREE
THE STORY OF THE PILL

Every day, millions of women around the globe pop a tiny pill in a blister packet – and in doing so assert their right to control their bodies, their sex lives and their reproductive destinies.

In March 2019, after suggestions that the contraceptive pill was waning in popularity in favour of less chemical options, the *Guardian* used the Freedom of Information Act to find out how many English women took it. They found that in the year 2017–18 almost 9 out of 10 women who received contraception from their doctor or pharmacy took either the combined pill or "mini pill" – a total of more than 3.1 million women.

The Pill had also hit the headlines two months previously. The UK's Faculty of Sexual and Reproductive Healthcare had released new guidelines on taking the pill, asserting that "there is no health benefit from the seven-day hormone-free interval" – a method of pill-packaging and prescription that had been in place since the drug's inception, causing millions of women to struggle through millions of completely unnecessary "periods". John Guillebaud, professor of family planning and reproductive health said the practice was "outdated", and introduced "arbitrarily" (in order to appeal to the Catholic Church) and could in fact reduce the effectiveness of the

Opposite: Members of the Parents' Aid Society campaign for the right to birth control outside St Patrick's Cathedral, New York City, *c.* 1965. The placard declares support for Bill Baird, a reproductive rights campaigner who was jailed eight times in the 1960s.

drug. Almost 60 years after its inception, the pill was back in the headlines again, but for all the wrong reasons.

Now considered to be one of the most significant medical advances of the twentieth century, the contraceptive pill – a seemingly magical combination of oestrogen and progesterone that prevents ovulation and therefore pregnancy – was first approved for release in 1960. This was the result of a years-long struggle by reproductive rights campaigners and enlightened medical practitioners, who advanced the novel belief that women should have absolute control over their own reproductive function – these included the founder of Planned Parenthood, Margaret Sanger, who was instrumental in her insistence that women needed a private, autonomous and easy method of preventing pregnancy. Within two years of its release, 1.2 million American women were using "the pill". In Germany and the

Opposite: Planned Parenthood support badge, c.1970. Founded in 1916, the organization continues to provide women with access to contraception, abortion and other essential services.

Below: Marcia Goldstein, Publicity Director of Planned Parenthood, holds up the organization's latest New York City bus advert, 1967.

YOU CAN DECIDE HOW MANY
CHILDREN YOU WANT
PLANNED PARENTHOOD CAN HELP
...with information on birth control
and infertility services
CALL 421-2290
PLANNED PARENTHOOD OF NEW YORK CITY 29 WEST 57 ST. NEW YORK, 1001

UK, the pill was available from 1961 (in the UK, it was prescribed on the NHS for married women only until 1967). In France it was legalized in 1967, with most other European countries following suit soon after.

It is hard to evaluate the colossal and wide-ranging societal changes the pill brought to women all over the world. Some credit the pill as instrumental in kick-starting the twentieth-century sexual revolution, aka the age of free love – women were now free to have sex outside of marriage without the fear that all that loving might result in an unwanted pregnancy, and when pregnancy was less likely, perhaps the need for the stability of marriage wasn't quite so great. The pill brought bodily autonomy to women, too, who now had absolute control over their own cycles, health – and reproductive destinies. It also levelled the playing field for women in further education and in the workplace, who could now have sex without the fear of a pregnancy interrupting their studies or career progression, just when things were starting to get interesting. It made women powerful, not passive. It made women, so far as sex went, like men.

The pill now exists in over 30 different forms and is taken by over 100 million women worldwide. Despite this, for 60 years women have struggled to retain the power and autonomy the pill has given them, with regular attempts to erode it by various government administrations around the world. The struggle isn't over yet. But it is a fact that the contraceptive pill has revolutionized the terms of debate over women's rights forever more – and that's one thing they can't roll back.

Opposite: 1968's *Prudence and the Pill* was an outrageous-for-the-time comedy film centring on five couples who were trying to avoid pregnancy by using the contraceptive pill. Hilarity ensues ... or not. It wasn't a success.

A SPORTIVE LOOK AT THE FERTILITY RITES (AND WRONGS) OF WESTERN SOCIETY.

WHO
SWITCHED
THE PILLS
WITH
THE ASPIRINS?

20th Century-Fox presents

DEBORAH KERR · DAVID NIVEN

in FIELDER COOK'S

Prudence
and the
PILL

A KAHN-HARPER PRODUCTION

ALSO STARRING
ROBERT COOTE · IRINA DEMICK · JOYCE REDMAN · JUDY GEESON · KEITH MICHELL · EDITH EVANS

| PRODUCED BY | AND | DIRECTED BY | SCREENPLAY BY | | | |
| KENNETH HARPER | RONALD KAHN · FIELDER COOK · HUGH MILLS (BASED UPON HIS OWN NOVEL) | | Color by De Luxe | Music Composed and Conducted by BERNARD EBBINGHOUSE | | Suggested For Mature Audiences |

ORIGINAL MOTION PICTURE SCORE ON 20th CENTURY-FOX RECORDS

66/71

1970

COME TOGETHER
THE SUMMER OF WOMEN'S LIB

The late 1960s and early 1970s saw the launch of the women's movement proper. It began with women everywhere rising up and sharing, testifying, marching and protesting. A new age had begun: women's liberation was about to shake the world.

After the Summer of Love came the summer of 1968. It, too, has gone down in history. 1968 was the summer both Martin Luther King and Robert Kennedy were shot dead. It was the summer of music festivals on the Isle of Wight and in Newport. It was also the summer of the Orangeburg massacre and Vietnam War protests, and student strikes in Paris, Belgrade and across Europe. An entire generation of young people were turning on, tuning in and dropping out – but they were also engaging with political activism. It was against this backdrop of sit-ins and demos that the second wave of feminism began in earnest.

The year 1968 was also the thirtieth anniversary of the huge TV event that was the Miss America beauty contest. As they had done every year since 1938, a bevy of grinning women were about to come together to sashay pertly about in swimsuits and answer pat questions about loving children and world peace. But this year, the feminists were waiting. And they were about to ignite a global movement.

Opposite: A demonstrator drops her bra into the "freedom trash can", set up for women to discard "instruments of female torture" including girdles, mops, saucepans and magazines. Contrary to popular myth, no bras were ever burned at the protest.

The New York Radical Women (NYRW) had their roots in other radical political organizations as well as college campuses. In the lead-up to the pageant, they called on women to join together to protest "the image of Miss America, an image that oppresses women in every area in which it purports to represent us", as well as the latent consumerism and racism (no woman of colour had ever been crowned Miss America) bound up with the contest. It was the NYRW who mobilized hundreds of women to convene at the pageant in Atlantic City, New Jersey. They held up homemade signs emblazoned with "ALL women are beautiful!" and "Can make-up hide the wounds of our oppression?". A "freedom trash can" was set up for women to chuck away beauty aids and bras (later misreported as a bra-burning,

and forever associated with the event). A banner saying "Women's Liberation" was unfurled. And that was it – the women's movement was on the world stage.

What became known as the women's liberation movement or "women's lib" hit the headlines and began to spread through the global public consciousness like wildfire. Around the world, beauty pageants were targeted for protests. In 1970, in London, women threw flour bombs at the televised Miss World contest, drowning

Above: The New York Radical Women's group plan their 1968 Miss America beauty pageant protest. Their actions made headlines globally and put the women's movement on the world stage.

out Bob Hope's stream of off-colour jokes with football rattles and defiant chants of "We're not beautiful, we're not ugly, we're angry!". In Antwerp feminist protesters interrupted the televised 1971 Miss Belgium contest by chanting "We are not cattle!".

All over the world women started coming together, forming collectives and setting up "consciousness-raising groups" in cities such as New York, London, Berlin, Paris, Dublin and Barcelona, and in Copenhagen, Oslo, Reykjavik and Milan. These had names like Redstockings, WITCH, and Bread and Roses, or simply had acronyms that reflected some version of Women's Liberation Movement. The topics up for discussion included equal pay, workplace equality, free contraception, abortion and free childcare.

The women's movement was getting organized. In 1969 the first American Women's Liberation Conference was held in Chicago. In February 1970 more than 600 women attended the WLM conference in Oxford. Other cities and countries followed. By March 1970 the National Organization for Women (NOW), founded by Betty Friedan, had 35 chapters in America, with others existing in all the major cities. In Denmark in 1971 a women-only summer camp was held.

On August 26, 1970, on the 50th anniversary of American women's enfranchisement to vote, an estimated 50,000 women marched down New York's Fifth Avenue, taking part in the NOW-mobilized Women's Strike For Equality, which asked for legal abortion, free childcare, and equality in the workplace. Other similar demos took place simultaneously in Boston, San Francisco and Washington DC. Once again, the shockwaves of the mass event sent out one clear message to women around the world: the second wave of feminism has begun.

Opposite: At the landmark 1968 Miss America protest, a woman gets creative explaining the way she feels about women's objectification in beauty pageants, with the help of a friendly sheep.

Above: Mobilized by NOW, on August 26, 1970, an estimated 50,000 women linked arms and blocked traffic as they marched down New York City's Fifth Avenue as part of the Women's Strike for Equality.

Above: April 1972 issue of of Brussels' radical feminist journal *Et Ta Soeur?* This issue contains a critique of the family and calls for the abolishment of the patriarchy.

Opposite: The Women's Strike for Equality celebrated the 50th anniversary of American women winning the right to vote, as well as serving as a symbolic gesture. Women ceased cooking, cleaning and working to "strike" for their rights.

Overleaf: The Strike for Equality brought together women who were discovering the burgeoning women's movement. *Time* called the demo "the largest women's rights rally since the suffrage protests."

SUSIE ORBACH

PSYCHOTHERAPIST, PSYCHOANALYST & WRITER

ON WHAT FEMINISM HAS DONE FOR HER

Feminism saved my life. No exaggeration.

I met my best – and lifelong – friends in the first Women's Studies programme in New York City in the 1970s and with them went on to question, think, grow and develop together new possibilities for us as women.

Inevitably, as women and as part of a large social movement, we were determined to share what we were discovering, so that others would have the chance to open up their own lives and those of their daughters, mothers, aunts and the men in their lives.

Feminism allowed us to take ourselves seriously. It wasn't easy. As we embarked on activities that had been unknown to us, whether contesting given roles or daring to do new things, we drew on the real and imagined support from each other as we braved what had felt so forbidden. We were excited to be traversing new terrains, to discover we could grow, challenge, develop unexpected strengths, manage our vulnerabilities and love in new ways.

Feminism and my friendships and political groupings, from The Women's Therapy Centre to Endangered Bodies and all the campaigns in between, have helped me to develop new thinking in psychoanalysis about women, about bodies, about the complexity and subtlety of human emotions and the damaging ways society is organized and needs to change. It has also enabled us to understand how the structures of class, identity, ethnicity and "femininity" live inside us and have to be continually engaged with and contested.

Above all, feminism has kept me curious: curious about who we are as individuals and who we are in friendships, relationships, in families of all kinds and in our work. Feminist ideas, longings and arguments are so well integrated into who I am (and sit alongside other social justice imperatives) that I am grateful to have been from my generation. I am delighted, too, to see a feminist resurgence among younger people who seamlessly bring concerns and actions around climate justice, racism, othering and gender preoccupations to this generation's politics. If only the world could hurry up and change!

MIND THE GAP
THE FIGHT FOR EQUAL PAY

The gender pay gap was one of the key issues taken up by the second wave feminists – it went to the heart of inequality between the sexes, and was easily measured in simple statistics. For the first time, it seemed, women were demanding recognition of their worth.

The summer of 1968 did more than ignite the second wave of feminism. It also stirred something in the female machinists at the Ford plant in Dagenham, UK, who had been informed that their jobs were being downgraded and designated as unskilled – putting them in the same pay category as the factory's janitors. They were also told that they would be paid 15 per cent less than the rate received by said janitors. So on June 7, 1968, they went on strike.

Through the 1960s, very little had been done to challenge the assumption that pay was gendered. The working women of the Second World War accepted a salary on average 50 per cent lower than their male counterparts; in 1968 the belief still held that men worked to support families and women worked for some extra pocket money.

In the late 1960s and early 1970s, women did not commonly work in STEM, nor did they sit on the boards of companies as CEOs – they were more commonly found in the typing pool. Nor were women airline pilots: they were stewardesses. Women resigned when they

Opposite: The Washington DC march for the Equal Rights Amendment on July 9, 1978, saw over 100,000 women demonstrating in purple, white and gold in homage to the original American suffragists.

got married. It was perfectly legal for companies to pay men more and hire men over women – and they did.

The Ford workers strike sent a ripple out across the UK. Secretary of State for Employment Barbara Castle intervened, securing the women a pay rise (to 92 per cent of the men's pay), and began work to push Labour's Equal Pay Act into law. Meanwhile, the National Joint Action Campaign Committee for Women's Equal Rights was formed and agitated for an equal pay demonstration attended by 1,000 people on May 18, 1969. That same year the British Government's Equal Pay Act passed, with a further act banning sex discrimination in employment, education and training following in 1975.

Above: Sewing machinists from the Ford plant in Dagenham outside the House of Commons, June 1968.

In 1970, Betty Friedan also successfully mobilized thousands of working women to strike for equality across the USA where the Equal Rights Amendment had stalled. Beginning promisingly as an amendment tacked on to the Civil Rights Bill, it had passed in 1972 – but by 1977 it had still not been ratified, with three states holding out. NOW was also working to correct the way that newspapers such as the *New York Times* listed its job ads. Previously its "Help wanted" section had jobs listed under either "For women" and "For men" – the process of de-segregation had started, but progress was slow.

In the USA, as elsewhere, women of colour earned even less than their white counterparts (as they still do) and were discriminated against on sex *and* race grounds. The civil rights movement of the previous decades had, in 1964, brought in legislation forbidding racial discrimination. Despite this, it continued to be an issue, and women of colour also had the battle against sex discrimination to fight. This issue was highlighted by the 1976 *DeGraffenreid v General Motors*

EQUAL PAY NOW

Equal Pay Day marks the day in the year when women start working for free in their country. In 2021, The Fawcett Society reported a UK gender pay gap of 11.9 per cent, an increase from 10.6 per cent in 2020, when they published a report highlighting the impact of the Covid pandemic on widening pay parity: 1 in 3 working mothers lost work or hours due to childcare. The Fawcett Society calculates that, at the current rate of progress, it will take another 60 years to close the gap in Britain. In the USA, the 2021 average gender pay gap was 18 per cent. For black women it is 63 per cent, and for Hispanic/Latina women, 45 per cent.

lawsuit, in which five black women workers alleged workplace discrimination on the grounds of both race and sex – which the court refused to allow them to combine.

In Iceland the women's movement was more successful. Focusing on equal pay as an attention-grabbing issue, the country's Red Stockings group got stories in newspapers and on radio stations about Iceland's low pay and workplace sex discrimination. Fuelled by the wave of publicity, they succeeded in the incredible feat of encouraging 90 per cent of the country's women to demonstrate their value on October 24, 1975, by going on a day-long strike from work and childcare. Women gathered together en masse to sing, talk and hold banners, while banks, factories and schools had to close, leaving men literally holding the children instead. What became known as the Women's Day Off did more than facilitate equal pay – it shifted Iceland to a new way of seeing. In 1980 Vigdís Finnbogadóttir became the world's first democratically and directly elected female president. She went on to serve 16 years in office.

Right: On August 20, 1976, a group of workers – mostly East African, Asian and female – from the Grunwick Film Processing Laboratories in London, walked out in protest against their working conditions and pay. Led by Jayaben Desai (pictured), the strike lasted for two years. The demands were never met, but the strike is remembered as a triumph for solidarity – workers of all backgrounds and genders came together to fight for the rights of migrant women workers.

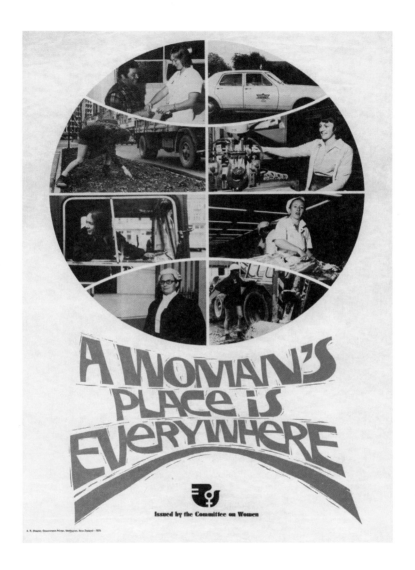

Above: 1975 poster for the New Zealand Labour Government's Committee on Women – aiming to establish a channel through which women could influence policy-making.

Opposite: Iceland's legendary Women's Day Off in 1975 is regarded as a seminal moment in the country's history. Iceland has ranked first for equality in the Global Gender Gap Index since 2009.

HEAR ME ROAR
FEMINISM HITS THE CULTURE

With the launch of the first feminist magazines, as well as the release of women's lib-themed pop songs, fashion pieces and advertising campaigns, the 1970s was the decade in which feminism exploded and took root in the zeitgeist.

The 1970s saw the new women's liberation movement transition from a political protest effort. Protests hit the headlines in newspapers, famous feminists appeared on magazine covers. Fashion went political. There was even a theme song. By the mid 1970s, it was hip to be a feminist. Women's lib had gone mainstream.

Part of this was because women's libbers were good at getting their message out. As soon as they had started coming together in the consciousness-raising groups, feminists had started producing things to communicate with – pamphlets and books, newspapers and journals. In 1970 a group of about a hundred women attempted a takeover of the *Ladies' Home Journal*, in an 11-hour siege that resulted in the male editor allowing the group an 8-page supplement in the August issue. In May 1971 France's Mouvement de Libération des Femmes (MLF) began publishing the feminist journal *Le Torchon Brûle*, printing 35,000 copies for its first run. In 1972 Gloria Steinem and others founded the glossy women's magazine *Ms.* – the first issue sold out in eight days and resulted in 20,000 letters and 26,000

Opposite: Spring 1971 issue of *Le Torchon Brûle* ("The Sparks Fly"). It was created by members of the MLF, including the artist Raymonde Arcier and activist Marie Dedieu.

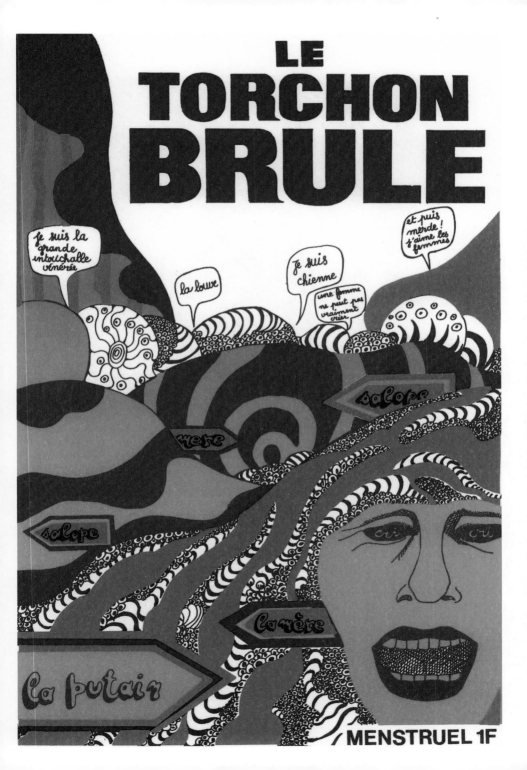

spare **Rib**

the new women's magazine
JULY 17½p

The days Women
rocked the World
Georgie Best on Sex
Does the Government
care about Pensioners?
Richard Neville
on the Glossies
Growing up in the
Bosom Boom

8 page News Section
and lots more inside.

Above: Issue 1 of *Spare Rib*, published on June 19, 1972. Provocative and clever,
the groundbreaking magazine addressed social and political issues as well as
including short stories and women's interest editorials.

subscriptions. That same year in Britain, a collective of women founded by Rosie Boycott and Marsha Rowe published the first issue of *Spare Rib*, which discussed feminist-slanted topics such as body hair, abortion and sex, all in a biting, irreverent style. *Spare Rib* would go on to be published for the next 21 years and become a publication that defined Britain's second-wave movement. Publications such as these helped the women's movement transcend meetings and protests and engage with every sort of woman – politically active or not – in their own homes.

The 1970s saw more mainstream publications incorporate feminist ideas in their editorials. *Cosmopolitan* magazine took the movement's message of sex positivity and ran with it, instituting beardy male pin-ups who had gold medallions glinting on luxuriant chest rugs, alongside contraception advice and tips for "successful lovemaking". Women on the *Cosmo* covers weren't just models – they were writers like Jilly Cooper and singers such as Helen Reddy, who in 1971 had released the song 'I Am Woman', which was to become the theme tune for 1970s feminism, with its lyrics of female empowerment. It was an anthem about being proud to be a strong, invincible woman, enough to roar about it, and never being held back again. No wonder it was an enormous hit.

On August 31, 1970, the feminist writer and activist Kate Millett featured on the cover of *Time*. Inside the issue, in an article entitled "Who's Come A Long Way, Baby?", the magazine referenced the famous tagline of a Phillips Morris & Co ad campaign launched two years before. This had used the exciting new women's liberation movement as a way to market Virginia Slims, cigarettes aimed specifically at women (their selling point being that they were tailored to a woman's hands and lips, and would fit neatly in your tiny feminine handbag).

Feminism too had permeated the echelons of fashion. The slogans of the movement became fashion items and pin badges. Labyris Books, the first women's bookstore in New York City, ran off T-shirts

printed with "The Future is Female", unknowingly creating a slogan that persists today. And though no bras were actually burned in the 1968 protest that ignited the women's movement, the discarding of bras – as well as the girdles and suspenders that had literally restricted women during previous decades of the century – became shorthand for the new movement of the 1970s. Just as trousers had once been emblematic of women's freedom, being braless seeped its way into the landscape of 1970s fashion. "Sisterhood is powerful" wrote Susan Brownmiller in a 1970 editorial in the *New York Times*. "Women's liberation is hot stuff this season."

By 1975 women's liberation was so mainstream that *Time* made its Person of the Year "American Women", declaring that "enough US women have so deliberately taken possession of their lives that the event is spiritually equivalent to the discovery of a new continent".

Opposite: Alix Dobkin wearing the T-shirt created by the Labyris feminist bookstore, which was in NYC's Greenwich Village.

Above: The cover of the preview issue of *Ms.*, first published as an insert in the *New York Times* in December 1971. Gloria Steinem was a staff writer on the paper at the time.

Overleaf: *Ms.* magazine staff meeting, New York City, 1975. Gloria Steinem can be seen back right, with founding editor Patricia Carbine in the foreground. *Ms.* is still being published today.

GISELA PÉREZ DE ACHA

JOURNALIST & ACTIVIST

ON BEING YOUNG AND QUEER
IN MEXICO CITY

I was 11, young and queer in Mexico City. No one ever told me about feminism. In my conservative Catholic school, I was asked to cover my body, go to Mass every day and marry young. My friends and I weren't allowed to play soccer. "It's for boys", they said, we had to behave like "ladies." But fitting in was not my thing.

I was a rebel. An erotic dissident. And a feminist.

At 21, I learned I was not the only one – there were hundreds of us, all around the world, pushing back on the dogmas that blamed us for getting harassed, that silenced us when we were raped, and ultimately prevented us from living freely in peace. I joined FEMEN – the topless warriors – to use my naked body as a political canvas. That was my introduction to feminism: postmodern, mainstream, pop and worldwide.

Fake news and Big Tech changed things around for me. All of a sudden, what had called me into activism became a problem in itself: dogmatic ideologies, withdrawn from facts and dissidents. Mexico needed accurate information, especially given that the media system was dominated by macho men in power, with little regard for gender-based coverage. Hundreds of stories were not being told.

It's 2020 and I'm 31 years old. The global #MeToo movement erupted around the world three years ago, and on International Women's Day, hundreds of thousands of feminist women took over the streets in Latin America. We inundated social media with videos and photos where we hugged and protested together, bearing green bandanas as the pro-abortion symbol, demanding the right to be free from violence and harassment.

I covered it as a journalist – a feminist journalist in one of the most dangerous countries to be one. Despite a stream of ongoing online harassment and threats, the force of sisterhood and the endless hope of keeping power accountable is what drives me forward.

After 20 years I now start to get it – feminism is a journey. I have healed the wounds of repression. I've found my voice through my writing. I have created around me a powerful and collective way of life. We are the fourth wave: pop feminism, backed by centuries of critical thought and analysis. We are the warriors, the rebels and the dissidents.

Mexico needs a radical transformation towards a safer and more democratic society, free from the grip of the narco cartels. Feminism as an ideology of peace, inclusivity and justice provides some essential basics to drive us towards it.

REPRODUCTIVE RIGHTS
THE BATTLE FOR WOMEN'S BODIES

The late twentieth century saw feminists engage in huge battles around abortion access, contraception and reproductive rights. The things that had held women back and repressed them were being overthrown and torn down, one by one.

Women have never stopped fighting for their reproductive rights. Since Margaret Sanger began her campaign to institute what became Planned Parenthood in the 1910s, debates around contraception and abortion have been cornerstones of the women's movement. Women have fought to gain control of their own bodies and reproductive destiny, as well as protect the most vulnerable in society. These issues, particularly, were touchpoints for the feminists of the 1970s, with many of the protests and conferences around the world focusing on abortion access as absolutely fundamental to women's true liberation.

For decades the illegality of abortion had not prevented it taking place, but rather meant that the operations were performed by unqualified professionals in less than ideal, even downright dangerous, circumstances. Many women travelled abroad to countries where backstreet abortions could be easily procured, or endured painful

Opposite: The Redstockings' flyer protesting the abortion reform hearing, in which a panel of "experts" consisted of 14 men and one woman (who was a nun). The group invaded and interrupted the hearing on February 14, 1969.

WHO ARE THE EXPERTS?

Today a panel of clergymen, doctors and other professional "experts" is picking apart the abortion law. They will tell us, in their usual daddy-knows-best manner, just how much control over our reproductive processes we should be allowed to have.

We say:

THE ONLY REAL EXPERTS ON ABORTION ARE WOMEN!

Women who have known the pain, fear and socially-imposed guilt of an illegal abortion. Women who have seen their friends dead or in agony from a post-abortion infection. Women who have had children by the wrong man, at the wrong time, because no doctor would help them.

Any woman can tell you:

Abortion laws are <u>sexist</u> laws, made by men to punish women.

LET THE EXPERTS TESTIFY.
SUPPORT CONSTANCE COOK'S BILL — REPEAL <u>ALL</u> ABORTION LAWS.

Women's Liberation Movement

procedures at home. In 1965, in the USA, illegal abortions made up one-sixth of all pregnancy-related deaths. Many countries offered few real alternatives to abortion beyond adoption, such as state-supported childcare or government funding.

The UK legalized abortion under certain circumstances in 1968. But the US held out on its women. Some thought the ratification of the Equal Rights Amendment was delayed due to the sense among conservatives that it was a gateway to abortion and gay rights. In

Above: An MLF demonstrator at a pro-choice march in Paris, 1972. Abortion was not legalized in France until 1975.

ABORTION DECRIMINALIZATION TIMELINE

1920 Soviet Russia (restricted in 1936 and legalized again in 1955)

1926 Germany (in cases of maternal health, illegal for Aryan women under Nazi rule but encouraged for non-Aryan women)

1931 Poland (re-criminalized in 2021, except in cases of rape, incest or health)

1935 Iceland

1936 Catalonia

1938 Sweden

1939 France (expanded in 1975)

1948 Japan

1964 Norway (made free to access in 1978)

1968 United Kingdom (expanded in 1990) excluding Northern Ireland

1969 Canada (expanded in 1988)

1969 Australia

1971 India

1972 East Germany

1973 USA (2021 severely restricted in some states, *Roe v. Wade* being undermined)

1976 West Germany

1977 New Zealand

1978 Italy

1980 Netherlands

1997 South Africa

2007 Portugal; Mexico

2009 Spain

2012 The Philippines; Uruguay

2018 Republic of Ireland

2019 Northern Ireland

2020 Argentina

2021 South Korea; Thailand

February 1969 a legislative hearing on abortion in New York City was interrupted when members of the Redstockings feminist group attempted to gain control of the microphone to testify about their own abortions. The following month they staged a public event encouraging women to share their experiences with abortion. Gloria Steinem covered the event for the *New York Times* and later said it was what made her "an active feminist". Steinem was to dedicate her 2015 memoir, *My Life on the Road*, to the doctor who risked the law to give her an abortion in 1957. "Dear Dr Sharpe, I believe you, who knew the law was unjust, would not mind if I say this so long after your death: I've done the best I could with my life. This book is for you."

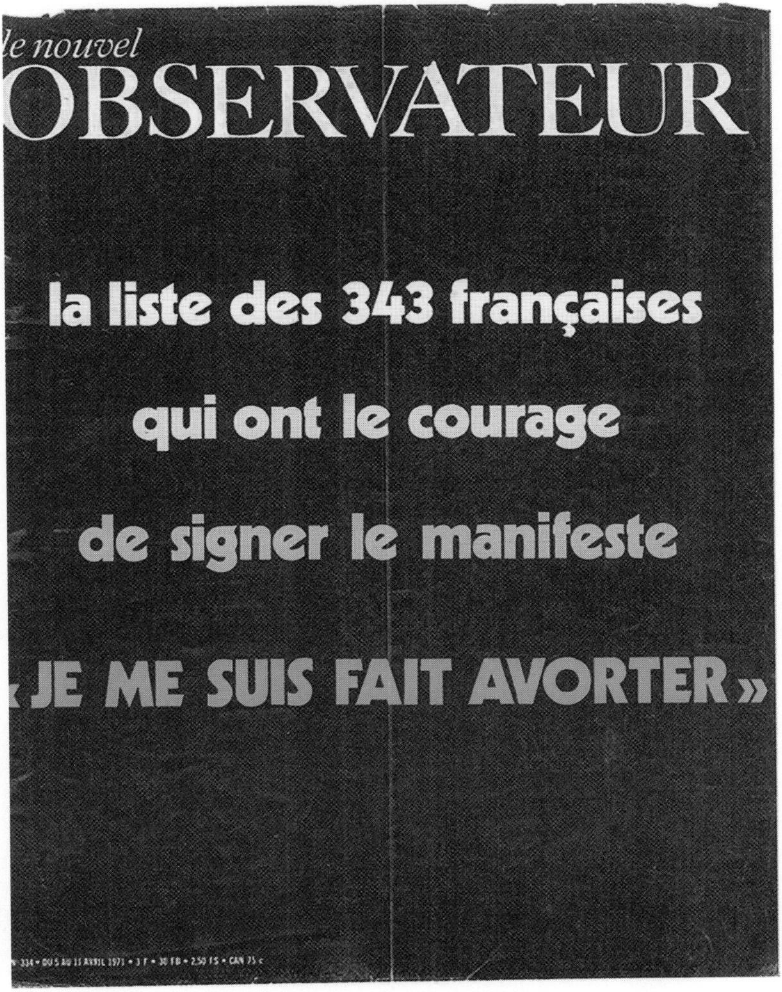

le nouvel
OBSERVATEUR

la liste des 343 françaises

qui ont le courage

de signer le manifeste

« JE ME SUIS FAIT AVORTER »

N° 334 • DU 5 AU 11 AVRIL 1971 • 3 F • 30 FB • 2,50 FS • CAN 75 c

Above: In April 1971 France's *Nouvel Observateur* published the Manifesto of the 343, which called for abortion access and free contraception.

Opposite: 1971 cover of Germany's *Stern* magazine. Inside, 374 women said they had had abortions. It is considered a landmark feminist moment in Germany.

Abortion was still illegal in France in 1971, when 343 women signed a public manifesto, authored by Simone de Beauvoir, to say that they had had an abortion. West Germany followed suit the same year with its own version, called "Wir haben abgetrieben!" ("We have had abortions!"), inciting the forming of pressure groups as well as the cross-city Aktion 218 campaign. By 1975 abortion was legal in France, and accessible in Germany, though it is still technically a criminal offence – in early 2022, the law was in the process of being reformed. In some countries, legislation does not equal access. Italy decriminalized abortion in 1978, though as of 2022, access is limited – nearly three quarters of doctors are registered "conscientious objectors" and exempt from performing abortions for religious or moral reasons – in Spain abortion was not decriminalized until 1985, and access is also severely limited in practice by conscientious objectors.

ROE V. WADE & DOBBS V. JACKSON WOMEN'S HEALTH ORGANIZATION

In 1973 Norma McCorvey (aka Jane Roe) began federal action against district attorney of Dallas County, Henry Wade. She argued that Texas law prohibiting abortion was unconstitutional in that it was a woman's right to terminate her pregnancy, supported by her right to privacy. McCorvey won the case, instantly overturning many state and federal abortion restrictions in a seminal turning point for the women's movement. In 2018 Mississippi moved to ban abortion beyond 15 weeks gestation. The state's only abortion clinic, Jackson Women's Health Organization, filed to block it on the grounds it was unconstitutional. In 2021 the now conservative-super-majority Supreme Court controversially announced it will hear Mississippi's appeal. A victory for the state would almost certainly mean a nationwide overturning of Roe v. Wade, with at least 21 and as many as 26 states poised to ban or severely restrict abortion access.

Above: Norma McCorvey, aka "Jane Roe", with her attorney Gloria Allred, at a pro-choice rally outside the US Supreme Court in Washington, 1989.

Overleaf: 1974 protest in Frankfurt am Main, West Germany, against section 218. The law criminalized abortion, with both the woman and the doctor going to prison.

QUEER IDEAS
DIVISIONS AND
ACCEPTANCE

Gay and radical feminists of the 1970s started conversations
about the way queerness and the women's movement intersected,
while emerging academics and thinkers introduced divergent
ways of considering feminism.

From the early days of feminism, queer women had struggled
to find their place within the largely white, heteronormative
confines of the movement. Despite the hot catchphrase of the second
wave – "the personal is political" – the 1970s saw growing criticisms
of the movement as too broadly white and middle class and ignoring
the different lived experiences of women of colour, lesbians, trans
women and differently-abled women, among other groups.

As the 1970s progressed, the initial optimism and mainstreaming
of women's liberation had given way to political divisions within the
movement. By the middle of the decade, radical – sometimes known
as revolutionary – feminists had emerged, who were exploring ideas
of separatist, women-only spaces and women-only initiatives. Some
radical queer feminists developed the idea of political lesbianism,
which called for all feminists to eschew having sex with men, which,
they believed was undermining the fight for women's liberation
and would assist with the problem of patriarchal culture, male

Opposite: Lesbian rights rally held at the bandstand, in Boston Common, 1974, still
a meeting point for pride and equality events and rallies today.

Above: Writer, feminist, poet and civil rights activist Audre Lorde, pictured in 1983 with a rousing feminist slogan.

domination and violence against women. The culmination of this saw the controversial booklet *Love Your Enemy? The Debate Between Heterosexual Feminism and Political Lesbianism* (LYE), which floated the idea of sexuality as a choice, published in Britain in 1981.

Among the radicals was Rita Mae Brown – who helped form the separatist lesbian group and Washington DC commune The Furies Collective. Brown led the Lavender Menace (later renamed Radicalesbians), a group who proposed absolute female separatism from men.

Elsewhere, feminist queer intellectuals and theorists, chafing at the second wave's rigidity concerning LGBTQ+ issues, became the varying voices of the queer feminist movement. Theologian Mary Daly – sometimes called the first feminist philosopher – was a radical feminist who challenged the idea of God as a man. The poet and essayist Adrienne Rich's more socialist feminist vision explored an alternative to a patriarchal system through her verse and activism. Lesbian poet and writer Audre Lorde advocated for feminism that spanned across age, race and class lines.

It was not until the 1990s that the term "intersectionality" would be formally introduced into scholarly feminist discussions. It had first been coined by civil rights scholar Kimberlé Crenshaw in a 1989 academic paper as a way of discussing how gender, race, class and sexuality overlapped with one another.

Towards the end of the 1970s, radical feminist conversations were moving from queerness to sexuality. Andrea Dworkin had begun to make a name for herself through her activism and writings opposing pornography, which she critiqued as being harmful in its focus on male dominance. The so-called "feminist sex wars" began when other sex-positive feminists rejected this idea as representative of censorship and ultimately, repression of women's sexual expression. Kate Millett wrote openly about her feminism and bisexuality, and was critiqued for it by some radical lesbian feminists.

PROMINENT TRANS WOMEN TO KNOW

Captain Hannah Graf (UK)

The highest ranking trans woman in the British army, Hannah Graf is a spokeswoman and mentor. In 2019 Stonewall named her Trans Role Model of the Year.

Janet Mock (USA)

A journalist-turned-bestselling-author and advocate, Hawaii-born Mock became the first transgender woman of colour to write and direct an episode of television in 2018.

Angela Ponce (Spain)

In 2018 LGTBQ+ activist Ponce became the first transgender woman to compete in the Miss Universe competition.

Paris Lees (UK)

Journalist and TV presenter Lees became British *Vogue*'s first transgender columnist in 2018 and the first openly trans presenter on Radio 1 and Channel 4.

Raquel Willis (USA)

This former national organizer for the Transgender Law Center, writer, journalist and activist Willis is now a spokesperson and the executive editor of *Out* magazine.

Tessa Ganserer (Germany)

A member of The Greens party since 2008, Ganserer became the first openly transgender person in a German parliament when she came out in 2018.

Andrea Jenkins (USA)

Jenkins became the first African American trans woman elected to public office in the USA when she won her seat as a member of the City Council in Minneapolis in 2017.

Vladimir Luxuria (Italy)

The first openly transgender member of Parliament in Europe, Luxuria became an LGBTQ+ spokesperson and TV presenter after leaving politics in 2008.

Laverne Cox (USA)
An actress and LGBTQ+ advocate, Cox rose to prominence for her role in *Orange is the New Black*. In 2014, she became the first openly transgender person to appear on the cover of *Time*.

Kim Petras (Germany)
One of the youngest people to undergo gender confirmation surgery at age 16, Petras – originally from Cologne – is now a singer/songwriter based in Los Angeles.

Raffi Freedman-Gurspan (USA)
The first openly transgender person to work as a White House staffer, Freedman-Gurspan was also the first transgender legislative staffer to work in the Massachusetts House of Representatives.

Rachel Levine (USA)
The US assistant secretary for health and a four-star admiral in the Public Health Service Commissioned Corps, Levine was the first openly trans government official to hold an office that requires Senate confirmation.

Nikkie de Jager (Netherlands)
This award-winning beauty vlogger and makeup artist has accumulated over 1.5 billion views with her platform of self-love and empowerment. In 2020, she was announced as a goodwill ambassador at the UN.

Jin Xing (China)
China's foremost transgender celebrity and the country's leading contemporary choreographer, Xing's incredible elegance as a dancer and actor, along with her popularity as a TV hostess, has earned her the title of "the Oprah of China".

Hunter Schafer (USA)
As well as her iconic performance as Jules on *Euphoria*, and the critically acclaimed episode that she cowrote, Schafer's LGBTQ+ activism landed her an interview with Hillary Clinton and a place on *Teen Vogue*'s "21 under 21" list.

Aoife Martin (Ireland)
An IT professional and trans rights advocate, Martin now campaigns and writes about trans issues in Ireland.

It was not until the 2000s that mainstream awareness grew of the issues faced by those feminists who identified as trans women, and who didn't subscribe to binary gender norms. High-profile trans women such as Laverne Cox, Janet Mock and Caitlyn Jenner helped the topic fast become a talking point among feminists. By the late 2000s, a section of the women's movement known as trans-exclusionary radical feminists or gender-critical feminists had emerged, mainly in the UK and USA, who believed that only cisgender women should be allowed to call themselves "women", and that trans women could not be oppressed by their gender in the way that cisgender women were. Gender critical feminism became particularly high profile in the UK, ignited by 2017 discussions around the Gender Recognition Act, a 2004 law establishing how trans people could amend the gender on their official ID documents, the issue then being picked up and discussed by the UK media and prominent UK feminists. The debate continues to inflame feminist discourse in Britain.

Opposite: Author and activist Kate Millett in 1989. Her book *Sexual Politics* (1970) discussed the relationship between the patriarchy and sexual relationships, and is a a key text of second wave feminism.

PERSONAL TESTIMONY

JUNO DAWSON

AUTHOR & SCREENWRITER

ON WHY TEENAGE GIRLS NEED
A NEW KIND OF FEMINISM

I spend a lot of time in schools and I often ask, "who defines themselves as a feminist?" Maybe three or four hands out of a hundred go up. Obviously this isn't enough. What part of their own freedom are these young women not sold on? I wonder if this is because feminist conversations often focus on quite adult concerns: marriage, work and pay. These are three vital elements of the feminist movement obviously, but ones which don't immediately apply to 11-year-old girls.

Similarly the number of female directors in Hollywood, female CEOs, and "male gaze" in cinema are simply not of interest to swathes of women and girls and yet we seem to have a lot of the same conversations among media types. Why? Because the women given a voice in the mainstream press are interested in those things. White, middle-class, cisgender and straight voices are overrepresented.

This, globally, has been summed up as "white feminism". Don't get me wrong: I am all of those things, except one: I am transgender. Struggling to get my voice heard – and failing to find content by women like me – has given me a kick up the bum. We need to apply mainstream feminism to the specific concerns of women from minority groups. Feminism, in my mind, is the tool we use to free women from whatever is holding them back. For some that will be racism; for others it will be deprivation, poverty or ill-health. For all of us, it's misogyny and patriarchy. For trans women, our struggle is compounded by continually having to defend our "realness" or validity; we may struggle to access healthcare; we are more likely to be sex workers. Many trans women are also poor, from minority ethnic groups or have disabilities.

If only a global handful of powerful, rich women are benefiting from feminism, it isn't feminism.

How does this relate to those 11-year-old girls? Well, they belong to all those groups too. We need girls to understand that gender is holding us all back, but some of us have greater obstacles than others. We need to teach them the value of supporting other girls and women. If one of us attains power, we can bring in other girls and women. We need to make them understand what bodily autonomy means and how patriarchal systems have always come for those rights to make decisions about our own bodies.

NOT EVERY WOMAN
ATTEMPTS AT INTERSECTIONALITY

Once the second wave was fully underway, it became clear that the new feminism had limitations – women of colour were underrepresented and their concerns were not reflected. Change began with activism.

T hough this was a decade in which the women's movement made great strides in the realms of equality, it had its limitations. In America, for one, where the collectives and consciousness-raising groups had been born on university campuses and in politically engaged circles, membership was skewed toward the white middle class. The term "intersectional" was not yet coined, though women of colour experienced the effects of being doubly oppressed by racism and sexism in a country that had engaged in both slavery and state-mandated racial segregation.

Betty Friedan's *The Feminine Mystique*, which had ignited the second wave, was also limited in its scope and spoke mainly to the anguish of white middle-class, suburban housewives. Unsurprising, then, that at the beginning of the decade, women of colour were conspicuously absent in direct-action campaigns and high-profile media coverage, seeming to fall between the cracks of the civil rights movement and white-dominated second-wave feminism. In her 1981 book *Women, Race and Class*, Angela Davis decried the lack of historical inclusion of

Opposite: Protester with badges during the Chicago Women's March for Equality on August 26, 1971. The pro-choice badges highlight how important that particular issue was to feminists of the time.

BRING U.S. TOGETHER

VOTE **CHISHOLM** 1972

UNBOUGHT AND UNBOSSED

N.G. SLATER CORP. 220 W.19 St.- NYC - 10011

Above: Activist, academic and writer Angela Davis in 1969, soon after she was fired from her job as philosophy professor at UCLA for her radical politics. She subsequently had a distinguished academic career and has become a world-renowned figurehead for black women's rights.

Opposite: The first black woman elected to the United States Congress in 1968, in 1972 Shirley Chisholm became the first woman and first African American to run for the nomination of a major party for president of the United States.

black women in feminist movements from the suffragettes onward, pointing out that class and racial divide was at the heart of the issue. "'Woman' was the test," she wrote "but not every woman seemed to qualify."

In May 1973 a group of high-profile black feminists came together to form the National Black Feminist Organization (NBFO). They included writers Alice Walker and Michele Wallace, artist Faith Ringgold, and activists Margaret Sloan-Hunter and Florynce "Flo" Kennedy – one of the first black women to graduate from Columbia Law School, who had founded the Feminist Party in 1971. The group of 30 NBFO members set out to raise awareness about the specific feminist issues that pertained to black women, such as poverty, sexual abuse and media representation. Their statement of purpose read, "The Movement has been characterized as the exclusive property of so-called white middle-class women and any black women seen involved in this movement have been seen as 'selling out', 'dividing the race', and an assortment of nonsensical epithets. Black feminists resent these charges."

With origins in the NOW, the NBFO organized discussion groups focusing on the interests of women of colour, including anti-domestic violence and sterilization campaigns, and pro-abortion demos and conferences. By February 1974 it had over 2,000 members and 10 chapters across the USA. The same year, the Combahee River Collective (CRC) came together as a breakaway from the NBFO Boston chapter. Founded as a more radical alternative to the NBFO, the CRC was a black lesbian organization that included women who were also Black Panther Party members, and who had decided on a more revolutionary socialist agenda.

Opposite: Poster for the November 1969 Connecticut protest in support of six female Black Panthers who were on trial for murder.

WOMEN! FREE OUR SISTERS

SIX of our black sisters, members of the Black Panther Party, are imprisoned on trumped-up charges in Niantic State Woman's Farm in Conn.

THREE are pregnant;
TWO will give birth before the end of 1969;
NONE HAVE BEEN TRIED OR FOUND GUILTY OF ANY CRIME

YET THEY ARE:
isolated from other prisoners;
kept awake by constant bright lights and noise;
denied their LEGAL right to choice of counsel;
denied their CIVIL right to choice of doctors;
denied their PHYSICAL right to exercise, fresh air and proper clothes;
denied their HUMAN right to their children;

And what these women are suffering is an extension and reflection of the conditions forced on all women, especially those of us who are black, brown, and poor and who say NO to THE MAN.
WE DEMAND freedom and self-determination for ALL women

WE REJECT: the State's definition of "fit" mother, family unit and "suitable" home. the State, by its torturous treatment of our Panther sisters has proven itself to be an "unfit" guardian for these children.
WE INSIST: that a mother is NOT "unfit" because she does not conform to repressive political, social, marital and cultural codes;
A FIT MOTHER WOULD MOVE AGAINST THESE CODES AS OUR PANTHER SISTERS HAVE DONE!

What these women are suffering is part of the repression the State is bringing down on the Black Panther Party;
The State is making sure that these children will be born into a hostile, brutal and racist environment;
The State is making sure that the Black Panther Party will not produce another generation of Panthers.

Since we recognize the Black Panther Party as the true representative of the people;
WE DEMAND with the mothers, that the Black Panther Party be allowed to care for these children as is the desire of the Black Panther men and women.
WE DEMAND immediate freedom for the Connecticut Panthers and for all political prisoners.
WE DEMAND an end to the isolation and sleepless nights.
WE DEMAND adequate diet, exercise and clothing.
WE DEMAND their right to choose counsel.
WE DEMAND their right to prenatal and maternity care by doctors of their choice.
WE DEMAND their right to give birth without armed guards.

Because the U.S. is waging a genocidal war of aggression against the Vietnamese people;
Because the U.S. is waging a similar war, with different means, against the black, brown and poor people;
Because the Vietnamese are fighting back and WINNING on their home front;
Because the black, brown and poor people are RISING UP on the domestic front;
Because women are STRUGGLING for the same things that all oppressed peoples are fighting for—

WE WILL SHOW THE PRISONS, THE COURTS, AND THE STATE THAT WE WILL NOT TOLERATE THE OPPRESSION OF OUR SISTERS ANYWHERE IN ANY WAY, SHAPE OR FORM

Sat. Nov. 22, NEW HAVEN

N.E. WOMEN's Liberation and the Black Panther Party of Conn. are calling for a massive demonstration to protest the "preventative detention" of the Conn. Panthers and in support of all political prisoners.
DOCTORS WILL BE WITH US TO DEMAND IMMEDIATE ENTRY INTO THE PRISON TO CARE FOR OUR SISTERS.

For further information please contact: N.E. Women's Liberation (749-5971 or 227-2617) The Black Panther Party of Connecticut, (203) 562-7463

please send contributions to: N.E. Women's Liberation, c/o Room 7, 2700 Broadway, NYC 10025 The Connecticut Panther Defense Fund, P.O.B. 7117, New Haven 06159

As the decade closed, the need for a new, intersectional kind of feminism was still a problem in the women's movement as a whole. As CRC member Barbara Smith wrote in 1979, "Feminism is the political theory and practice to free all women: women of color, working-class women, poor women, physically challenged women, lesbians, old women, as well as white economically privileged heterosexual women. Anything less than this is not feminism, but merely female self-aggrandizement."

Above: Women of the Black Panthers and Women's Liberation Movement shout "Free Bobby! Free Ericka!" as they march in New Haven, Connecticut, November 1969. The charges were eventually dismissed.

ANNE WAFULA STRIKE

PARALYMPIAN WHEELCHAIR
RACING ATHLETE & CAMPAIGNER

ON A MORE INCLUSIVE
FEMINISM

I was born in Mihu, Kenya. When I was two-and-a-half, I contracted polio. We were ostracized from our village. It was a traditional African setting where there wasn't enough education and awareness of my condition. We had to flee to Nairobi. I lived in a culture where men were superior to women, and a woman with a disability was at the bottom of the pile. But my father taught me feminism because he believed I was equal to everybody else in this world. He made me reach for the stars and supported me all the way to university. I graduated as a teacher, which was big news in Africa, for a disabled woman, in the mid-1990s. Coming to the UK in 2000, I realized I had three things that stood in my way: I had a disability, I was female but also I was black. I'm constantly having to push these things aside.

Sometimes I ask myself: what kind of feminist am I? I believe in all of us working together. I feel that the feminism movement has left me, as a disabled woman, behind because my voice is rarely amplified when it comes to so many things. In my TED Talk I asked, "Where is the voice of the disabled woman? Who is on the streets and demonstrating on behalf of the disabled women?" Disabled women suffer from low self-esteem because society is throwing barriers at them. How do we work with the women's movement to bring disabled women into discussions and boardrooms? I want to redefine feminism. To me, it's about equity and inclusion. It shouldn't be racist or sexist or just for women. When you're running a handicap in a race, the fastest will start from 350 metres and the slowest will start from 150 metres, so at least there's a possibility of them finishing together. To me, that is what feminism is. We need to take into consideration the challenges that other groups of people face. Feminism should include everyone, with all of our differences.

FREE LOVE?
SEX AND THE FEMINIST

After the pill came the sexual revolution. For the first time, women were freed from the expectation of marriage and children. That left them free to have careers, cohabit, and enjoy lots and lots of sex.

As a new generation put flowers in their hair and drifted down Haight-Ashbury in the late 1960s, it was a sign the structures of relationships were changing. The sexual revolution had introduced the concept of "free love" – which in real terms meant that women, specifically, were beginning to have sexual experience before marriage. Helen Gurley Brown's bestselling manual *Sex and the Single Girl* (1962) had got the ball(s) rolling, suggesting that a life beyond marriage represented one of glamour, fun and freedom – and lots of sex. Experimentation with polyamory, group sex and what was known as "swinging" began to emerge. The *New York Times* reported in 1968 on the brand-new trend that was "cohabiting", noting that contraception – specifically the pill – was facilitating the new trend. By the 1970s, women were questioning the structures of marriage that seemed to represent the opposite of freedom.

When it came to women's rights around marriage in the first half of the twentieth century, progress had been slow. In daily life, particularly the domestic sphere, women's inequality was starkly apparent. Women left home to move in with their husbands. Even

Opposite: A couple hanging out at the Woodstock Festival in August 1969. Woodstock has become emblematic of the "free love" hippy movement that defined the sexual revolution of the 1960s.

VATICANO
SACRA ROTA
BASTA!

L.I.D.

BARI L.I.D.

10.000.000
BASTANO?

SI
DIVORZIO

NO AI DIVORZI DELLA CHIESA
A SUON DI MILIONI.

BARI

in the 1960s, being a single woman after the age of 25 was to risk lifelong spinsterhood. Upon marriage in the early 1970s, women were still expected to give up education and work, and devote themselves to keeping house, cooking, chores and childrearing, the latter of which was expected to happen continuously throughout a woman's childbearing years, whatever her health or the couple's financial circumstances. Women in dire financial straits had no abortion access, with no way out of an unhappy or violent marriage to boot. In

Above: Helen Gurley Brown, author of *Sex and the Single Girl* (1962), which gave advice on sex, men and affairs. On publication it sold 2 million copies in 3 weeks.

Opposite: Members of the League for Divorce demonstrate for the introduction of the divorce law in Italy, July 14, 1970. Despite opposition from the Catholic Church, the law permitting divorce was passed in December of that year.

the early 1970s divorce was still rare and socially unacceptable and, in most Western countries, difficult to obtain.

For a woman, getting into marriage was easy – the legal age was based on puberty in many countries – but getting out of it was hard. Divorce, too, was usually based on "fault". Most countries required the proving of adultery or abandonment, which in reality was expensive and complicated. For women, divorcing without their husbands' consent was difficult. Legally severing abusive marriages was almost impossible.

The burgeoning women's movement had ignited debate around equality and marriage law reform. In 1969 the UK introduced the Divorce Reform Act, which allowed for the grounds of "irretrievable breakdown"; divorce on the grounds of domestic violence was not extended until 1976. California became the first state to introduce no-fault divorce in 1969, and over the 1970s state after state followed suit.

Across northern Europe, the 1970s saw fault grounds similarly eradicated. Sweden led the charge, simplifying divorce in 1973 – no fault, consent or long separation was required. In Europe's Catholic countries the divorce issue was complicated by religion; Italy's legalization of divorce in 1970 provoked widespread public protests both for and against the legislation; Spain did not allow divorce until 1981; Irish women had to wait until 1995.

Unsurprisingly, the 1970s was the decade when divorce rates soared. By 1980 it was at a record high in the US. Women, too, were realizing that they had choices beyond marriage. In 1977 there were an estimated 1 million cohabiting couples in the USA (the real number was almost certainly much higher), the birthrate for unmarried women soared, and by the time the 1970s closed, women were free to make choices other than marriage. The 1980s looked hopeful, and bright.

Opposite: A couple getting it on in their tent during the Isle of Wight Festival on August 30, 1969 at the height of the hippy scene. The late 1960s saw women freed by the introduction of the pill to have sex outside marriage.

1980s

SMASHING
THE CEILING
EQUALITY IN THE WORKPLACE

The decade that made consumerism cool also saw women making professional strides. But despite the popularity of high-flying women on screen, the reality for the 1980s women who tried to "have it all" was quite different.

T he 1980s was a decade that, in many ways, was all about money, and therefore all about work. The Western world had just about adjusted to the notion of women's permanent role in the workplace, though in many countries equality and equal pay were still a work in progress. Professions, for one, still seemed to be divided along gender lines. Women's jobs were too often unskilled, as those tended to be more flexible when it came to working family-friendly hours. As the 1980s began, if women worked, it was still in hair salons and restaurants, or as typists, cleaners and shop assistants, while men had "careers". Regardless, the decade became one in which women began to strive toward the brand new concept of "having it all".

This cultural shift was enhanced by the fact that in many countries, newly elected conservative governments and booming globalization brought with it a swing toward consumerism and conformity. The "yuppie" culture was all about climbing the corporate ladder, and conspicuous consumption while you were doing it. This was the

Opposite: The film *9 to 5* (1980) was a workplace comedy offering women the satisfaction of a chauvinist boss who gets his just desserts and a happy ending involving equal pay and an office crèche.

decade of flash sports cars, massive perms, enormous brick phones and designer labels that screamed upwardly mobile.

In some ways this mobile attitude benefited women. The 1980s saw the numbers of women going into higher education soaring – as well as the number of women being represented in male-dominated professional fields such as medicine, law, business and accounting. In the US, by 1981, one-third of law students were female – a decade previously it had been 10 per cent. In 1984 the *New York Times* reported that the percentage of women in banking and financial management jobs had risen to 39 per cent, up from 9 per cent in 1960.

This increased representation meant that in the 1980s women were marrying later than ever before, and having children in their 30s. Some of them were even deciding to remain – gasp – single. Though

Above: Tyne Daly and Sharon Gless played *Cagney & Lacey*, a cop show with a groundbreaking – and overtly feminist – twist: the detectives were women.

Opposite: Despite equal pay and sex discrimination legislation passed by many countries, the gender pay gap persisted and women spent the 1980s continuing to fight for their rights in the workplace.

most feminists agreed true equality depended on childcare provision and legislation, the idea of companies automatically offering flexible working arrangements and shared parental leave was a distant dream (except in a few forward-thinking European countries such as Sweden, which had introduced free state-run childcare in 1975).

A new female ideal emerged, one in which women expertly juggled high-powered careers alongside marriage and children, all while "power dressing" in a skirt-suit and stilettos. But the stereotypes remained. In 1983, when Sally Ride left the Earth's orbit in *Challenger* to become the first American woman in space, the Stanford-educated doctor of physics met a barrage of questions from the media, later recalling she had been asked about her make-up, whether she cried when something went wrong, and if she would wear a bra in space.

The films and TV of the era similarly reflected the decade's new obsession with high-flying women in the workplace. This was the age of soaps and serial dramas set in hospitals, police stations and law firms. In the 1980 film *9 to 5*, three secretaries in the form of Dolly Parton, Jane Fonda and Lily Tomlin take revenge on their sexist pig of a boss. Beginning in 1982, *Cagney & Lacey* saw two undercover female police detectives breaking new ground, with the portrayal of women battling home life and a sexist workplace. In 1987's *Baby Boom*, Diane Keaton becomes the ultimate "having it all" icon, transforming from archetypal 1980s corporate-career bitch to a loving mother who sacrifices her chance at the big time to fit her cutesy new baby-food-making job around family life. *Working Girl* in 1988 charted the rise of an ambitious working-class secretary with big business dreams. "I have a head for business and a bod for sin", the line immortalized by Melanie Griffith, encapsulated the complicated vision of femininity that emerged in the decade.

Opposite: Starring Diane Keaton as a hotshot yuppie who gives it all up for accidental motherhood, 1987's *Baby Boom* embodied the era's confused message about women who "had it all".

Overleaf: First US woman in space Sally Ride on the space shuttle *Challenger*, June 1983. NASA expanded astronaut selection to include women in 1978.

PEACE IN THE VALLEY
THE WOMEN OF
GREENHAM COMMON

Modelled on the spirit of sisterhood learned in the previous decade, the camp created at Greenham showed the world that mass female-centric eco protesting was not only possible – it could be powerful.

Nineteen years after it was first set up to protest nuclear arms, in September 2000, arguably the world's largest, most high-profile and longest-lasting active feminist protest came to an end. The Greenham Common Women's Protest Camp was formed in August 1981 by 36 feminists, all of them concerned about the dangers of the Cold War and planned nuclear waste disposal sites. Coming together under the name Women for Life on Earth, they set off from Wales to walk the 120 miles (195 km) to Greenham Common military base in Berkshire, England. It was sited on an area of common land that had been appropriated by the British Government after the Second World War. Their action was prompted by the decision to locate 96 American Tomahawk nuclear cruise missiles on the Greenham site – part of a NATO strategy to disperse hundreds of missiles across Western Europe.

The women delivered a letter to the base commander stating their concerns, and established a "peace camp", despite the lack of shelter or facilities. They created makeshift shelters from tarpaulins and tree branches, and dossed down in sleeping bags, lit campfires and decorated the site with ribbons and flowers. In an attempt to draw more media attention to their cause, some of the women chained

Above: Made by Thalia Campbell, this "Remembrance Is Not Enough" banner was used in the huge march against nuclear weapons on Remembrance Sunday 1981, and then displayed on the Greenham perimeter fence.

themselves to a perimeter fence. Women from all over the world seemed to feel the pull of this all-female space, and this new, female-centric approach to war protest – even those who had not previously engaged in activism. The group's numbers grew and grew. The Ministry of Defence, aided by the police, attempted to remove the women, beginning forcibly by driving bulldozers in to demolish the makeshift camp. This ended in arrests and imprisonment, as it had done decades earlier for the suffragettes, generating similar images of protesting women being physically assailed by law enforcement.

The attempts at dispersal only served the Greenham protesters' cause, and numbers further swelled. By 1982 the camp was in the

global spotlight. An estimated 30,000 women converged on the site for the action they called "Embrace the Base". They surrounded the perimeter, pinning baby clothes and other female symbols to it, while singing, and pulling and pushing at the perimeter fence, toppling it in places, to the bewilderment of attending police officers. When the missiles arrived in 1983, thousands of women around Britain showed their support for the Greenham camp through the Star Marches, organized by local groups.

Above: On December 12, 1982, thousands of women formed a "chain of peace" around the Greenham base perimeter, marking the first year of protest.

Above: For many women who came to join the camp at Greenham, it was the first time they had ever protested.

Opposite: Activist Sarah Green holds her baby, Jay, the first baby to be born in a tent at the peace camp, in 1983. He was registered as Jay Greenham in honour of the event.

Greenham Women Against Cruise Missiles

3,000 women blockade USAF base, Greenham Common, England. December 13, 1982

Center for Constitutional Rights Legal Education Pamphlet

What happened at Greenham Common proved to be a catalyst for other female-centric protest groups. It had shown that women coming together in non-violent action could effect change. The mass camp has been remembered as a positive example of feminist cooperative living, which was queer and intersectional. Eco-feminism had been rising in the late 1970s and early 1980s, and Greenham seemed to express the political mood that was in the air for the women's rights movement. However, some criticized the eco-feminist standpoint, which equated women with nurturing, nature and peace, and could be seen as reductive or, indeed, so anti-patriarchal as to be separatist. In the USA in 1980, 2,000 women came together to protest, following an accident at the Three Mile Island nuclear power station. The statement from the Women's Pentagon Action read, "We are gathering at the Pentagon on November 17 because we fear for our lives. We fear for the life of this planet, our Earth, and the life of our children who are our human future."

In 2015 Beeban Kidron, the director of the documentary *Carry Greenham Home*, wrote, "Greenham was a place where a generation of women found a public voice. It was a voice that was predicated on inclusion and difference, multiple perspectives not a single dominant view." That voice was important. Feminists were entering a new age of self-expression.

Opposite: The NYC-based Center for Constitutional Rights sued on behalf of the Greenham women, claiming the missile deployment violated international law as well as the US Constitution. *Greenham Women Against Cruise Missiles v. Reagan* was unsuccessful.

ART IS A
FEMINIST ISSUE
POLITICAL EXPRESSION
VIA CREATION

As feminism became a part of the culture, so too did feminist art, with women artists increasingly exploring political issues, and moving beyond basic feminist themes into representation, race and identity.

L ike their proto-feminist forbears who had craved a room of their own and freedom from domestic worries to pursue art, so the women of the 1980s communicated their politics and ideas through the creation of art – but this time they could be overtly, ragingly, extravagantly feminist. Not that feminists making art was a new thing. From the days of the early suffragists and their branded colour schemes, feminists had communicated their ideas through the visual arts with posters, slogans, graphics and painting. By the mid-1970s film, photography, sculpture, collage and other mixed media, as well as performance art, had also come to the fore, as women attempted to navigate the new landscape of society through new forms.

In 1971 the art historian Linda Nochlin had published a rallying call in the form of her essay *Why Have There Been No Great Women Artists?*, which argued that women's creativity had been restricted by the role mapped out for them by society, by the literal restrictions

Opposite: *Untitled (You Are Not Yourself)*, 1982, by Barbara Kruger. In the 1980s Kruger began collaging found, mass-media images to comment on female stereotypes in advertising and popular culture.

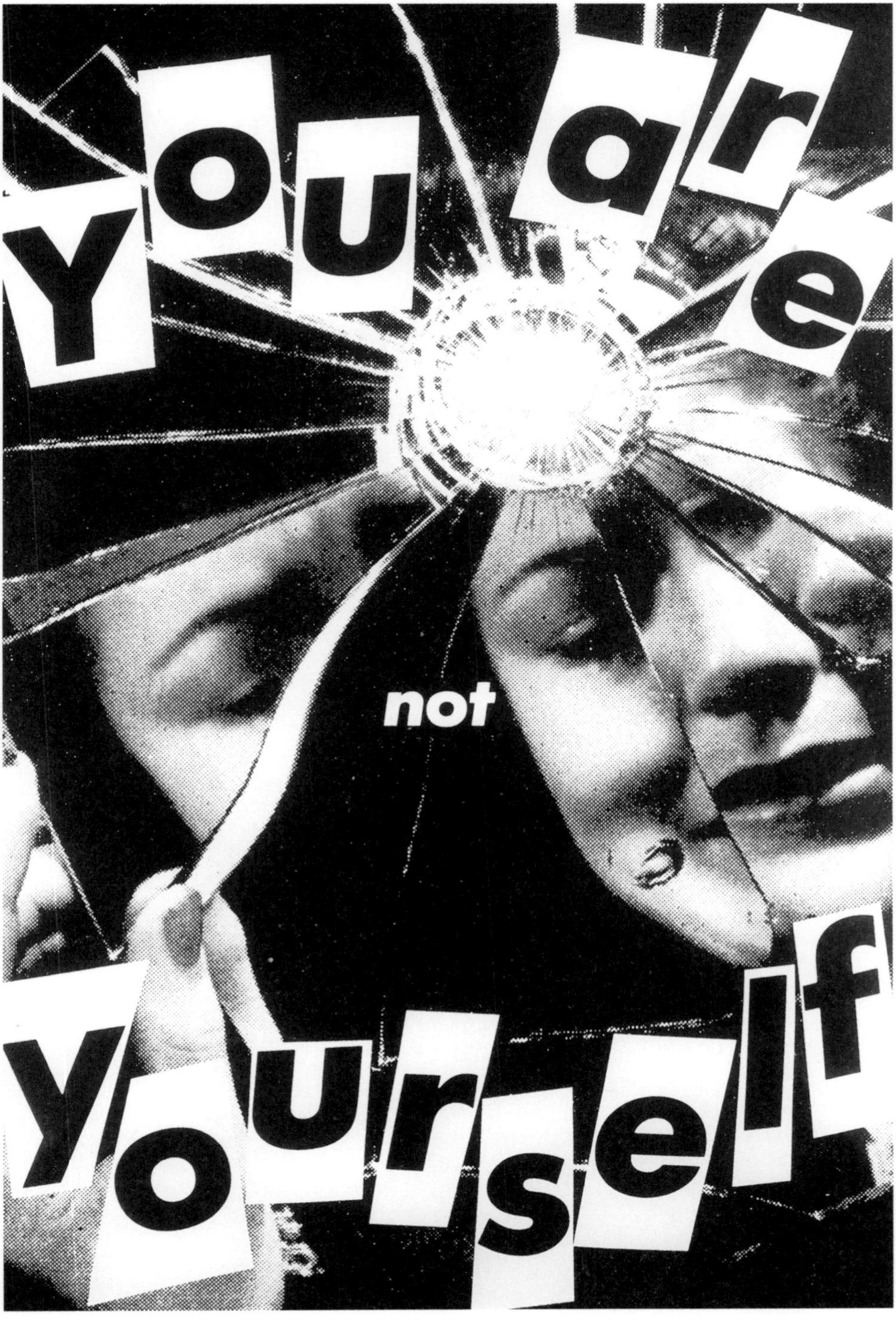
You are
not
yourself

cookin' & smokin'

where we at
Black Women Artists 1972

Carol Blank   Kay Brown   Carol Byard   Gilbert
Jerrolyn Crooks   Iris Crump   Pat Davis   Doris Kané
Mai Mai Leabua   Dindga McCannon   Onnie Millar
Charlotte Richardson   Faith Ringgold   Ann Tanksley
Jean Taylor

Exhibits at Weusi-Nyumba Ya Sanaa Gallery

158 West 132nd Street —— Harlem - New York
Opening January 2, 1972 — 3:00-7:00 P.M.
Closing January 20, 1972
Gallery Hours: 6-10 P.M.
Telephone 283-9475

Above: Excluded from the mainstream art world, the 1970s saw women artists of colour forming their own collectives. Where We At was formed in Brooklyn in 1971 by Dinga McCannon, Faith Ringgold and Kay Brown. This poster advertises their group show.

Opposite: *The Dinner Party*, 1979, by Judy Chicago. Considered to be a defining work in the feminist art movement, this large-scale installation celebrating women's history and achievements drew 100,000 visitors when it first went on display. It continues to be a site of feminist empowerment and conversation.

of childbearing and motherhood. In 1981 Griselda Pollock and Rozsika Parker's *Old Mistresses* went further, calling for the feminist reappraisal of art history. By the 1980s, women's art had taken flight.

The subjects and inspirations for this art were manifold and diverse. Some, like the women artists who had come before them, turned their eyes inward: to their perceptions of their bodies and their feelings about beauty; to their sense of themselves in relation to typically feminine characteristics; to the objectifying and stereotypical representation of women in art; and to perceptions of the male gaze. Others gave voice to the traditionally female areas of domesticity, relationships, sex and motherhood, or lack of it.

The modern art scene in particular was becoming increasingly politicized. Judy Chicago's *The Dinner Party*, completed in 1979, lit up the scene with its critique of women's representation in a patriarchal history, and created a monument to their accomplishments in the

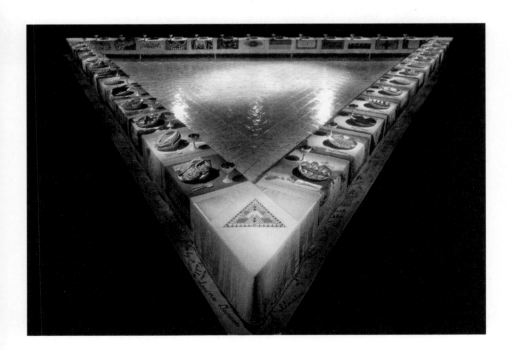

form of a huge triangular table including place settings for 39 women, each commemorating an important woman from history. Other 1980s artists who took up the baton included Jenny Holzer, who used large electronic signs to make statements such as "Abuse of power comes as no surprise"; Barbara Kruger collaged advertising to explore constructions of gender; and Cindy Sherman used self-portraiture to critique media representation of women.

The 1980s, too, saw women of colour putting race and identity at the heart of their art-making. The exhibition Where We At Black Women Artists, Inc. – held in the spring of 1971 – was an important precursor, drawing attention to the whitewashing of the art scene. The women artists of the 1980s went further and became more visible, as more women rose to senior positions in galleries. The 1989 series

ve to be naked to he Met. Museum?

n 5% of the artists in the Modern Art sections are women, but 85% of the nudes are female

Statistics from the Metropolitan Museum of Art, New York City, 1989

GUERRILLA GIRLS CONSCIENCE OF THE ART WORLD

Zabat by Maud Sulter, the mixed-media British artist and writer, was produced in direct response to the lack of black representation at other exhibitions. Her large-scale colour photographs featured powerful portraits of creative women of colour, including herself. Sulter was one of 11 women artists featured in The Thin Black Line, a landmark exhibition at London's ICA in 1985, which positioned contemporary black and Asian women artists as important players in the British modern art scene. Women were becoming more visible.

Above: Formed in New York City in 1985, and still active as of 2022, The Guerrilla Girls is an anonymous collective of feminist women artists that highlights gender inequality and racism within the art world. Wearing gorilla masks for public appearances, the group creates posters, stickers, books and video, as well as staging actions.

BEYOND THE DINNER PARTY
FOUR TRAILBLAZING FEMINIST ARTWORKS

Things Are Not Always What They Seem: Spirit Creature for the Afterlife of Little Black Girls (2018)
Vanessa German

The self-taught "citizen artist" Vanessa German works across sculpture, painting and performance art, her community involvement informing much of her work. *Things Are Not Always What They Seem: Spirit Creature for the Afterlife of Little Black Girls* is a piece from her 2018 exhibition of "power figures" – large-scale sculptures made from found materials – resembling minkisi, the spiritual effigies of the Kongo people. *This piece*, using toys, flowers and crystal, responds to the criminalization, sexualization and vulnerability to sexual abuse and violence of black girls in America.

My Bed (1998)
Tracey Emin

Her art seems to embody the feminist slogan "the personal is political" and *My Bed* was one of the readymades that brought Tracey Emin fame. Nominated for the 1999 Turner Prize, *My Bed* is the result of Emin's epic, four-day, bed-based heartbreak bender, and features her dirty sex-stained sheets, tissues, blood-stained knickers, empty vodka bottles, contraceptive pill packets, cigarette butts and used condoms. A landmark of feminist art, *My Bed* serves as a commentary on female stereotypes and a confessional, autobiographical portrait of a woman's life in the late twentieth century.

Womanhouse
(1972)

Judy Chicago and Miriam Shapiro A huge collaborative experiential piece, *Womanhouse* took place in a condemned house in Hollywood, and was visited by an estimated 10,000 people over the course of a few weeks. Twenty-one students from the Feminist Art Program (FAP) at California Institute for the Arts renovated the house then art pieces were installed and staged within it, transforming the space from a domestic sphere into "a place of dreams and fantasies". Pieces examined female stereotypes around domestic roles and beauty standards, including Chicago's *Menstruation Bathroom* and Shapiro's *Dollhouse*.

The Picnic at Giverny
(1991)

Faith Ringgold Combining stories, personal narratives, history and politics, Faith Ringgold's story quilts combine the traditional female techniques of quilting – which Ringgold learned from her grandmother, who was born into slavery – with folk paintings and story books. *The Picnic at Giverny* depicts a group of women in Monet's Giverny garden, gathered around a nude Picasso, who is posing on a blanket for a black female artist, reversing the traditional roles of painter and muse, as well as the idea of the male gaze in art. Part of the artist's French Collection, the piece offers a feminist revisionist view of the early School of Paris.

ROSIE WOLFENDEN

CO-FOUNDER OF TATTY DEVINE

ON MAKING FEMINIST
JEWELLERY

Our jewellery has always been about self-expression. At first, it was about enabling ourselves and others to have a way to show individuality and to kick against the bland, homogenized world that globalization was inducing. But in 2013 we noticed a lot of women asking for name necklaces saying "Feminist", so we decided to make some. It was the start of something big. We were amazed at how controversial this word was and how ready it was to be decoded. There was a new generation of women with information at their fingertips and ready to take action.

It was around this time that we met Lucy-Anne Holmes, who launched the "No More Page Three" campaign. She asked us to make necklaces using the slogan and, in the tradition of the suffragettes, Tatty Devine campaign jewellery was born. Since then we have watched the gradual shifts around gender equality, the disruption to social conditioning and the very slow disentanglement of that invisible and archaic structure that suppresses and holds women back – the patriarchy.

In 2018 we started working with the Fawcett Society, the UK's leading charity campaigning for gender equality and women's rights, covering issues from equal pay to anatomy not being a destiny. As a way to donate money and support the charity, we designed jewellery to celebrate the year of the woman and the first ever sculpture of a woman to grace Parliament Square, which, unbelievably, was also the first in the square to be created by a woman, artist Gillian Wearing. The brains behind this was Caroline Criado Perez, who campaigned to make this happen and is a constant source of inspiration.

Jewellery is a powerful way to spread messages: it empowers the wearer by giving them a medium in which to be political. The realization that people, women especially, were extremely open to wearing jewellery that expresses their views was a revelation. Whether by chance or choice, we have created a platform to campaign from and we intend to keep doing so until we reach our number one goal – equality.

MASSIVE SHOULDERPADS
DRESSING FOR POWER

They were a key part of women's professional dress and allowed them to not only feel more confident and powerful, but to literally take up more space. All hail the iconic 1980s shoulderpads.

W hen we think of the landscape of women's fashion in the 1980s, one thing stands out: the shoulderpads. Not since the Second World War had shoulders been so prominent in the silhouette of women's clothing, and never have they been again. Shoulderpads were everywhere in the 1980s. They were strutted down the catwalks of powerhouse designers such as Italy's Armani and France's Thierry Mugler. They were key in adding to the high camp and theatricality of soapy American TV melodramas such as *Dallas* and *Dynasty*. Shoulderpads were suddenly to be found in every fashion store, in every garment on the rack: they were in blouses, they were in dresses, they were in jumpsuits and they were in coats. They were really, especially humongous in coats.

Shoulderpads were a key part of the 1980s women's style that has gone down in the fashion annals as "power dressing". The look was representative both of the "dress for success" consumerist culture that had gripped the age and of the evolving role of women following the explosion of the women's liberation movement in the 1970s. This

Opposite: Joan Collins in 1980. Collins' trademark look was loud, tailored and shoulderpadded – emblematic of the trend that was sweeping fashion.

was partly because women in the workplace, and in more senior jobs and professional fields, needed a uniform with a powerful, more masculine emphasis, so that they could be taken seriously at work and feel confident appearing like "one of the guys". Shoulderpads not only had the bonus of making women literally take up more space in the office, they gave the handy illusion of masculine broadness to female shoulders.

The 1980s working woman's uniform consisted of (shoulderpadded) skirt-suits and pantsuits, with a waisted (shoulderpadded) blouse, perhaps with a pussybow in place of a tie – teamed with pointy stilettos, to keep things on the right side of feminine. This dressing diktat was followed by many prominent career women of the age, among them Margaret Thatcher, who had become Britain's first female Prime Minister in 1979 and is remembered for her trademark boxy, blue, shoulderpadded jackets, and her pussybow blouses.

The ideal female shape was changing in the decade, as gym fitness and aerobic workouts – as well as the cult of plastic surgery – exploded. Suddenly, sculpted athletic physiques were all the rage, as was fitness fashion such as leotards, shiny leggings and legwarmers, worn à la *Flashdance*. Madonna was an early adopter of the underwear-as-outerwear trend, which projected both exaggerated femininity and an insouciant sex-positivity. This was also to be found in her lyrics and those of her contemporaries, such as the punkier Cyndi Lauper, who wrote clever songs with a distinctly female viewpoint, such as female masturbation banger 'She Bop', about a woman who just can't stop herself from having a bit of a fiddle.

Opposite: Celebrity women including Grace Jones, Princess Diana, Oprah Winfrey and Jerry Hall were proud wearers of the shoulderpad, the 1980s look which allowed women to project confidence and literally take up more space.

Overleaf: Models wearing Armani suits, 1982. Giorgio Armani was one of the fashion designers instrumental in transforming 1980s' women's silhouettes, adapting the power suit for the yuppie age.

Though hemlines were rising and miniskirts, body-hugging spandex and leggings were all big news, so too were tomboy looks that allowed the new generation of second-wave feminists to dress freely and comfortably, in blazers and bombers, preppy slacks and shorts, and brogues. Strong female icons who wore their tailoring with pride included Grace Jones, Annie Lennox, Barbara Walters and Oprah Winfrey, all of whom gave women empowering sartorial inspiration.

The decade's rollercoaster of social and political change was reflected in the wave of women's political fashion designers that came up in the 1980s. Katharine Hamnett was at the forefront of the slogan T-shirt trend when she met Thatcher in 1984, unzipping her jacket to reveal a tee that read "58% don't want Pershing" – a reference to nuclear missiles. Elsewhere, subversive punk labels like Bodymap twisted gender norms and elevated style that had emerged from subculture and the punk aesthetic, which itself had mushroomed out of the alternative nightclub scene. Boys had perms, lipstick and eyeshadow, and girls had dungarees, brogues and bomber jackets. Sartorially speaking, in the 1980s equality had happened. But elsewhere, it was a different story.

Opposite: In 1984 Katharine Hamnett met Margaret Thatcher at Downing Street. Her T-shirt slogan was a response to Thatcher's decision to allow US Pershing cruise missiles to be stationed in Britain.

HANDBAGS
IN THE HOUSE
PARITY IN POLITICS

The decade in which women took their places in governance, justice and lawmaking was also one of rising conservativism. Was the 1980s as much of a boom time for women in politics as it seemed?

A generation of women came of age in the 1980s. Many of them were eager to get into politics and governance, having been part of the second wave's campaigns and protests movement. They were helped in practical terms by increased female access to education and workplace equality legislation. This was partly tactical: the women's liberation movement had recognized that true change would be brought about only when women were in place as lawmakers and legislators, as chief justices and ministers, as presidents and prime ministers. The problem was getting a seat at the table. In the 1980s politics was basically one big boys' club. Everywhere.

The culture and structure of many governments had always been – and by the 1980s, was very much still – historically and exaggeratedly male. Many parliamentary debate chambers were aggressive and combative. Moreover, in practical terms, political jobs were demanding, especially in an era that was still getting to grips with equality on the domestic and workplace front. The hours of many parliaments were

Opposite (clockwise from top): The female faces of 1980s politics: Diane Abbott, Lesley Abdela, Ruth Bader Ginsburg, Geraldine Ferraro, Indira Gandhi, Gro Harlem Brundtland and Margaret Thatcher.

OUR
COMMON
FUTURE

FERRARO
for America

not compatible with family life (in the UK until 2012, all Parliamentary sessions were from 2.30 pm until as late as 11 pm, and sometimes later). To date in the UK, cover for MPs seeking maternity leave is not provided. (My own MP Stella Creasy became the first woman to organize a "locum MP" to cover her constituency work while she took parental leave in late 2019. In 2021 she launched This Mum Votes, a scheme to get more mothers into politics, after she was told it was against the rules to bring her baby into the House of Commons.

Some trailblazing women of the 1980s were breaking into top elective offices, which might seem like women were achieving representation in the places where it mattered most – at the heart of law and policy-making. In fact, during the decade, a significant proportion of women struggled to take their places in governments around the world. Yes, women were making some huge leaps: Britain had its first female prime minister, the handbag-wielding Margaret Thatcher, who served from 1979 until 1990 (but though an endearing icon of female power, it should be noted the Iron Lady was most definitely not a feminist, promoting only one woman to her cabinet in her 11-year term, and she was decidedly uninterested in promoting women's issues); Britain's first black female MP came in the form of Diane Abbott (elected in 1987); India had Indira Gandhi; Iceland had Vigdís Finnbogadóttir and Norway had Gro Harlem Brundtland. American women may well have been cheered by the 1981 appointment of Sandra Day O'Connor as the first female Supreme Court Justice in United States history (the next woman, Ruth Bader Ginsburg, would not join her until 1993), and by the appearance of Geraldine Ferraro as the first woman vice presidential candidate for a major party.

These women whose names have endured were the exception not the rule. Governments around the world had serious gender-

Opposite: Newly appointed first female Supreme Court Justice Sandra Day O'Connor outside the Supreme Court in Washington, 1981. She served until her retirement in 2006.

parity issues in their law-making bodies. A striking case was France, despite the country's history of feminism and political protest – where women had been able to vote only since 1944, representation in political office in the 1980s was almost unbelievably low, and even by 1996 women made up only 6 per cent of National Assembly members. Many countries took steps in the decade to address these issues of underrepresentation. Sweden blazed a trail, introducing a system of proportional representation which greatly boosted women in political office (as of 2022, 46 per cent of Sweden's parliament were women, the highest in Europe). In 1980 in Britain, the all-party The 300 Group was formed by Lesley Abdela, inspired by the 1979 election that swept Margaret Thatcher to power but elected only 18 other women (or a paltry 3 per cent of parliament). The 300 Group held workshops, conferences and training courses for women who wanted to be political candidates; at its height it had 5,000 members and 40 local chapters throughout the UK. As the 1980s closed, organizations like The 300 Group were changing the conversation, but there was still a very long way to go.

Right: Vigdís Finnbogadóttir in 1980, the year she was elected president of Iceland, making history as the first elected female head of state in the world. At the time female political participation in Iceland was 5 per cent – in 2021 it rose to 47.6 per cent. In 2021 Iceland celebrated its twelfth consecutive year of ranking first in the Global Gender Gap Index, which ranks countries according to how close they are to reaching gender equality.

HOW SPAIN CHANGED THE GAME

In May 2019, when Spain's newest cabinet was sworn in (pictured above), it was a historic moment. Prime Minister Pedro Sánchez, created the first majority women cabinet in European history, appointing women to 11 of 17 positions. This was the result of gradually increasing representation from the 2000s – in 2004, Socialist Prime Minister José Luis Rodríguez Zapatero, created the country's first gender-equal cabinet of eight women and eight men. Then in 2007, the Spanish Socialist Workers' Party administration – a longtime advocate of women's rights in Spain – passed a quota-based gender equality law requiring party election lists to be at least 40 per cent female.

In 2019, Finland's Sanna Marin – the country's third female PM and, at age 34, the world's youngest head of state – broke Spain's record when she introduced a cabinet that was 61 per cent female. In 2021, Albania introduced its first female majority cabinet with 12 of 17 female ministers. Globally, only Rwanda (61.3 per cent), Cuba (53.2 per cent) and Nicaragua (53.1 per cent) have higher female representation in government. In 2021, though, only 21.9 per cent of government ministers around the world were women. In 2021 the World Economic Forum estimated that at the current rate of progress it will take 145.5 years to attain gender parity in politics.

BEING SEEN ON SCREEN

THE AGE OF FEMINIST FILM

From experimental art film to documentary, drama and comedy,
women filmmakers rose up in the 1980s to discover new forms of
cinematic – and political – expression.

Women's liberation had, by the 1980s, provoked a need for films that gave women more hearty fare than the romantic comedies, slushy weepies or melodramas that were being made for them, by men. Female directors had been in the extreme minority in Hollywood since the dawn of the silver screen, but in Europe women were supported by state funding and a tradition of experimental forms, and it was emerging as the heartland of feminist cinema.

As women sought to record their experience, documentary emerged as one of the earliest forms. The late 1970s saw films such as *Song of the Shirt* and *Daughter Rite*, which played with the documentary form as they expressed a visual ideal that was eminently female. Both were shown at 1979's The Women's Event at the Edinburgh Film Festival, one of the first such events to focus entirely on the work of female filmmakers. Connie Field's 1980 film about the working women of the Second World War, *The Life and Times of Rosie the Riveter* mashed archival footage with present-day interviews. *Not a Love Story*, directed by Bonnier Sherr Klein and released by the feminist film production agency Studio D, critically investigated pornography's role in society from a distinctly feminist perspective.

Above: Poster for director Helke Sander's *Die allseitig reduzierte Persönlichkeit –
Redupers* (1977), now considered to be an important film in the German feminist
film canon. Sander made several films in the 1980s dealing with feminist themes.

In Germany, the 1970s had seen a rise of women filmmakers. Margarethe von Trotta was directing films that engaged with contentious German political issues, featuring female protagonists and seeming to portray the emerging feminist idea that "the personal is political". Von Trotta's solo debut, 1979's *The Second Awakening of Christa Klages*, explored female relationships and female violence, a theme she returned to in 1981's *Marianne and Julianne*, which portrayed two siblings fighting for different kinds of rights. With 1986's powerful biopic of the socialist freedom fighter Rosa Luxemburg, von Trotta ensured her place in the New German Cinema movement and as a prominent feminist filmmaker.

Helke Sander, who had been part of the second wave's Bread and Roses feminist group, organized the first feminist film conference, in West Berlin, and headed up her feminist film journal *Frauen und Film*.

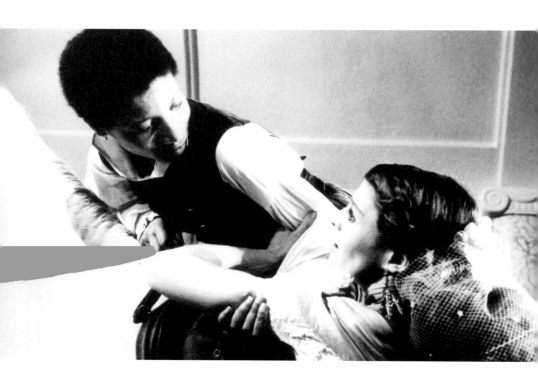

Above: Sally Potter in 1997. The British director became known as a feminist filmmaker in the 1980s and went on to direct *Orlando* in 1992. She continues to make experimental cinema.

Opposite: Colette Laffont (L) and Julie Christie (R) in Sally Potter's *The Gold Diggers* (1983).

Overleaf: Still from Agnès Varda's 1985 film *Vagabond*, which offered a new kind of female protagonist – one who drifts through France as an outsider, attempting to resist gender roles and societal norms.

In 1977 Sander made *Die allseitig reduzierte Persönlichkeit – Redupers (The All-Round Reduced Personality)*, in which the complicated and demanding lives of women living in West Germany were explored. In 1989's *Die Deutschen und ihre Männer – Bericht aus Bonn (The Germans and Their Men – Report from Bonn)*, she merged fiction and documentary, and made waves with the subject matter, investigating the impact of the women's movement by interviewing German men from all walks of life, with entertaining results.

Meanwhile, with her playful and political depictions of femininity on screen, Agnès Varda had spent the 1960s at the epicentre of the French New Wave. She was always a filmmaker who had been interested in notions of gender, and in the 1970s her interest in feminist themes deepened. Varda made the documentary *Réponses de Femmes (Women Reply)*, and in 1977 she released the feminist musical *One Sings, the Other Doesn't*, which explored themes of women's friendship as well as agency over their own bodies. Several other feature films followed. By the 1980s Varda had begun to sharpen her political viewpoint, creating less whimsical, more powerful depictions of women, such as her powerful story centring around a homeless woman in 1985's *Vagabond*.

The feminist film movement of the 1980s saw the industry reassessing what women wanted from film, as well as provoking a new generation of women to try to create cinema that reflected their burgeoning awareness, needs and concerns. And it gave them jobs – perfectly exemplified in Sally Potter's 1983 film *The Gold Diggers*, which not only explored feminist themes but had a groundbreaking, all-female cast and crew. By the end of the decade, Hollywood was getting to grips with the new trend for woman-centric cinema. There was *Desperately Seeking Susan*. That was a start.

Opposite: Rosanna Arquette and Madonna starred in 1985's hit female-fronted comedy, *Desperately Seeking Susan*, directed by Susan Seidelman, about a woman who breaks free from a stifling marriage to discover her creativity.

MAKING SPACE
WOMEN AND THE BUILT ENVIRONMENT

As the 1970s moved into the 1980s, women architects and planners realized feminism was empowering them to think differently about the spaces they lived in. Enter a new age for female-centric building design.

Caroline Criado Perez rose to prominence in 2013 when she successfully campaigned for a female historical figure to appear on British banknotes. In 2019 she published a bestseller: *Invisible Women: Exposing Data Bias in a World Designed for Men* takes on town planning, zoning laws and public transport. All are designed, the book posits, around male lifestyle needs by default, and do not take into account women, who are more likely to perform caring roles and undertake local commutes. Housing estates, she points out, are still being built to accommodate parking for cars, rather than playground areas for children. The ever-present threat of violence against women is still not being incorporated into design of public spaces such as transport stations.

These ideas were all born in the late 1970s and early 1980s when the women's movement impelled women to link their feminism with the built environment. In the mid-70s, movements like Reclaim the Night in the UK and Take Back the Night in the US had seen women

Opposite: Austrian architect Margarete Schütte-Lihotzky designed the Frankfurt kitchen in 1926. Efficient, affordable and hygienic, the kitchen rationalized housework and was the first fitted kitchen to be made in any quantity.

reclaiming urban spaces in which they felt unsafe and marginalized. The creation of Britain's Women's Aid in 1974 had brought with it the need for safe buildings in which women could escape domestic violence. In London it was also a boom time for public services and structures, supported by the Greater London Council (GLC), which began supporting feminist initiatives. The GLC formed a dedicated Women's Committee in 1982, which in turn set up research, seminars and guidance on the need for progressive female-friendly attitudes in urban design.

By the late 1970s, women architects, planners and builders were not only joining together to discuss the lack of female representation in the industry (in 1978, 94.8 per cent of architects were men), but also the lack of women's input during research and consultation, as well as the effects of gender bias on urban design that disregarded the needs of women and the differently abled and took conventional views of gender roles in spaces like the home. Some of these were more obvious problems such as hallways too narrow for prams, while others were more subtle: blind alleys in town centres that could be intimidating and dangerous.

In 1978 the Feminist Design Collective formed, some of whom created the Matrix Feminist Design Co-operative in 1980 – one of the first overtly feminist architecture practices in Britain. In 1984 they published *Making Space: Women and the Man-made Environment*. In it, the women explained feminist design was not about "curving buildings" versus "phallic towers" – it was about taking women's experiences, needs and lifestyles into account. The designer of the 1926 Frankfurt kitchen, Margarete Schütte-Lihotzky, was one of several early female architects who contributed groundbreaking ideas to the design of domestic spaces. But the built environment, the

Opposite: The age-old problem of navigating the built environment, particularly stairs, with children in tow.

Above: Matrix Feminist Design Co-operative was founded in 1980 – design by women for women.

Opposite: Pamphlet published by the Women's Design Service on women's safety on housing estates – a perennial issue.

WOMEN'S SAFETY ON HOUSING ESTATES

Published by Women's Design Service

new feminist architects argued, contained messages about prescribed gender roles and designs based on priorities decided by men, while housing plans reflected the oppression of women (in the early 1980s, houses were still being designed with cramped kitchens and large front rooms which assumed a nuclear family). Matrix carried out research and social design projects and offered technical advice.

Also powered by GLC grants, the Women's Design Service (WDS) was a research collective founded in 1987 by a group of women architects, designers and planners with the aim of helping women's groups with their building and space needs – such as the Jagonari Women's Educational Resource Centre in East London. They wanted to find less aggressive, more co-operative ways of working, and explore the ways male-dominated urban design failed women. They focused on toilets, crèches, housing, parks, pavements, safety and transport. When the funding began to dwindle under the Conservative government, the WDS established themselves as a research body as well as a source of information for public bodies. They published pamphlets, including the child-space-focused *It's Not All Swings and Roundabouts*, and advised London's new IKEA store on child-friendly areas. Their most famous publication, *At Women's Convenience*, was published in 1990 and included a research report and design guides on the hot topic of women's toilets, which, as Criado Perez highlighted 29 years later, is still a worldwide global issue.

Opposite: East London's Jagonari Women's Educational Resource Centre funded by the GLC, and designed by Matrix, opened in 1987.

1990s

REBEL GIRLS
THE RISE OF RIOT GRRRL

With its potently political feminist lyrics and anarchic punk spirit, the Riot grrrl music scene of the early 1990s made its mark on pop culture by advocating a new kind of feminism: one that was fearless, angry, and set to the thump of a driving bassline.

In America's Pacific Northwest something was brewing underground in 1990. Women on the alternative music scene were reaching for ways to express themselves about the then-male-dominated punk scene, their antipathy to the consumerist culture that created the previous yuppie decade, as well as ongoing national debates over women's reproductive rights. In Olympia, Washington, Kathleen Hanna, Billy Karren, Kathi Wilcox and Tobi Vail had formed a band, calling themselves Bikini Kill. Frontwoman Hanna remembered in 2013, "We were told that feminism didn't exist anymore; that there was no reason for it to exist because women had equality. I lived in a small town and had worked in the domestic-violence shelter, where I saw first-hand that equality for sure did not exist ... Those women were my inspiration."

Bikini Kill were overtly feminist, and not afraid to scream it: they put out a self-recorded cassette demo, *Revolution Girl Style Now*, featuring spiky, cut-and-paste punk anthems including 'Suck My Left One' and 'Double Dare Ya', the latter a manifesto-like call for women

Opposite: Kathleen Hanna fronting Bikini Kill during Rock for Choice 1993 in Hollywood. Hanna said the "Kill Me" dress was a comment on violence perpetrated against women, and what constituted "asking for it".

to: "Dare you to do what you want/ Dare you to be who you will/ Dare you to cry, cry out loud." Other bands heard the call, and soon there were other women howling their displeasure into the mic; like Oregon's feminist zine-producing Bratmobile, Olympia's Heavens to Betsy (whose vocalist and guitarist Corin Tucker would later go on to form Sleater-Kinney), and the UK's Huggy Bear. Soon there was a name for this blistering, bass-driven, feminist punk music, which was fronted by women in band T-shirts, kilts and loafers, who wore plastic bows in their hair and daubed "SLUT" over their bellies with marker pen. These bands wrote lyrics that called out sexual harassment, male entitlement, lack of female representation and sexual objectification, layered over music that was self-taught, raw, and really fucking loud. They advocated for a new kind of feminism, one that was really angry about quite a lot of things, and unafraid to express itself: these bands wanted revolution. They wanted riots. This was Riot grrrl.

When Riot grrrl bands played live, as they soon were doing all over coastal America and the UK, it was a safe space for women to unite

Left: Bikini Kill's 1991 demo cassette *Revolution Girl Style Now* signalled the birth of what was to become "Riot grrrl".

Opposite: L7 performing at the inaugural Rock for Choice at the Hollywood Palladium on September 27, 1992.

SIX ROCKING RIOT GRRRL ANTHEMS

Bikini Kill
'Rebel Girl' (1993)

Perhaps the ultimate Riot grrrl anthem, 'Rebel Girl' is a thundering, guitar-pounding song about revolution, rebellion, good clothes and friendship from the pioneer band of the movement.

Sleater-Kinney
'Little Babies' (1997)

Taken from *Dig Me Out*, the album that took Sleater-Kinney mainstream, 'Little Babies' is a joyful 2:22 burst of brilliance with a catchy chorus that's all about the stereotype of women as caregivers.

Babes in Toyland
'Bruise Violet' (1992)

The second single from the band's first major label album, *Fontanelle*, 'Bruise Violet' is a thumping slice of thrash punctuated by lead singer Kat Bjelland groaning the word "liar" for the chorus.

L7
'Pretend We're Dead' (1992)

With lyrics expressing the ultimate apathy and the blistering riff opening that will have you reaching for your air guitar, L7's commercial hit is part moshing anthem, part celebration of women who rock.

Bratmobile
'Cool Schmool' (1993)

Lo-fi and homemade-sounding in the very best way, 'Cool Schmool' is a shouty garage rock stomp of a song by the band that also brought you the original Riot grrrl bible aka *Girl Germs* fanzine.

Heavens to Betsy
'My Red Self' (1991)

Starting as a melancholic, stripped-back song about period shaming, this understated banger features Corin Tucker singing the immortal lines "Is this the rag/ You use to humiliate me/ 'Cause I was born/ I was born a girl?" A Riot grrrl classic.

Opposite: Carrie Brownstein, Janet Weiss and Corin Tucker, aka feminist punks Sleater-Kinney, who came together in 1994 in Olympia.

Above Minneapolis band Babes in Toyland, who formed in 1987, inspired many Riot grrrl groups that followed.

in their rage against the machine; to cut loose, and crowd surf, without fear of harassment or harm. Riot grrrls pogo-d on stage and thrashed their distorted guitars – and then encouraged you to buy their homemade DIY fanzines with editorials that spoke out intelligently against "the general lack of girl power in society as a whole, and in the punk underground specifically" (*Riot Grrrl* fanzine, July 1991).

By the mid-90s the Riot grrrl baton had been taken up by other alternative female-fronted, feminist-orientated bands, and Riot grrrl hit the mainstream. L7 brought the "fuck you" ethos to the masses, throwing their tampons into the crowd at a festival and showing their fulsome bushes live on TV, while Sleater-Kinney brought the personal and political to the late-90s grunge landscape. Then there were Babes in Toyland, Veruca Salt and Hole. By now Riot grrrl was becoming diluted: women's music was less focused on the political; the Spice Girls repackaged "girl power" for themselves. Nevertheless, Riot grrrl persisted in the form of Kathleen Hanna's electroclash outfit Le Tigre, and post-Riot grrrl bands like Gossip and Pussy Riot. In 2016, the UK's Skinny Girl Diet launched their lo-fi, feminist, 1990s-referencing sound, ensuring Riot grrrl is embraced by a whole new generation of women. And this time they have smart phones.

GIRL POWER?
THE ERA OF EMPOWERMENT

From supermodels and ladettes to sassy superheroes and the Spice Girls – the 1990s was the decade of women celebrating themselves. But not everyone agreed on what "girl power" meant.

T he 1990s saw new and different – and often confusing – visions of femininity emerging, some of which seemed to directly contradict each other. The invention of the "supermodel" saw the likes of Claudia Schiffer, Cindy Crawford, Naomi Campbell and Linda Evangelista transformed into major-league celebrities, setting new impossible beauty standards in the process. With the rising popularity of porn and porno culture, "lads' mags" and the revival of the Playboy brand, bosomy blondes like La Cicciolina, Pamela Anderson and Anna Nicole Smith smouldered all over newsstands. The creation of 24-hour rolling news coverage, combined with a boom across pop music, television and print, meant scantily clad celebrities were everywhere. Media portrayals tackling feminist themes, such as Amy Heckerling's 1995 game-changing portrayal of the teenage girl experience in *Clueless*, were thin on the ground.

In the UK, thanks to positive discrimination, women's representation in the Labour Party surged with 101 women elected in the party's

Opposite: 1995's *Clueless* had themes of female friendship and empowerment as well as strong, sassy and opinionated female protagonists.

Overleaf: Linda, Cindy, Naomi and Christy during the finale of the Versace A/W 1991 runway show, which ushered in the new age of the supermodel – and a new set of impossible beauty standards.

landslide 1997 victory (somewhat demeaningly dubbed "Blair's babes" by the media), by far the most female MPs ever to enter parliament in one election. At the same time, a brand-new term was being coined by the British press: a "ladette" was a lass who behaved like a lad. Sweary, fearless and rebellious; she drank pints and fell out of nightclubs. In the UK, new celebrity presenters such as Amanda de Cadenet, Denise Van Outen, Sara Cox and Zoe Ball were photographed messily drunk and splashed all over the front pages.

The energy of the Riot grrrl scene and the rising feeling that a fresh kind of feminism was in the air had made the early 1990s feel exciting and full of possibility when it came to women's choices and identity. In the USA, the confident approach of black all-girl rap groups like Salt-N-Pepa and the hip-hop/R&B trio TLC, as well as the rise of female MC artists including Missy Elliot, Lil' Kim and Queen Latifah, were bringing feminist ideas to fans of pop music. Creating anthems that called out slut-shaming, domestic violence and abuse, they celebrated female independence, sexuality and ambition.

By the time the Spice Girls bounced into the world's collective cultural consciousness in the summer of 1996, with their Buffalo platform trainers, crop tops and V-signs, the "Girl Power!" message they carried with them reflected the new infectious, rebellious, feminism-infused spirit that the 1990s seemed to be about, and be more than just a canny antidote to a chart dominated by boy bands.

In the post-80s landscape, a return to political feminism had emerged. The Spice Girls may have been the mainstream, accessible and commercialized version of that vision, but were nevertheless still about confidence, liberation, sisterhood and having fun.

Opposite: Kick-ass on-screen women, clockwise from top left: Xena, Scully, Buffy, Catwoman and Sabrina all embodied dynamic female power.

Overleaf: The Spice Girls in 1997. Sporty, Scary, Baby, Ginger and Posh introduced a new generation to the notion of "girl power", and helped the idea catch on all over the world.

"There is a new attitude; girls are taking control," said Mel C in a 1996 *Big Issue* interview. And Victoria stated, "We're up for equality, for having a laugh." The Spice Girls' songs and videos, moreover, reflected a move away from manufactured, sexualized imagery that characterized mainstream 1990s pop – girl power was about dressing for yourself (which might mean lipstick, schoolgirl bunches and thigh high boots, or a tracksuit and trainers). Each Spice Girl had her own character. She was outspoken and real, and had acne or a pot belly, but still felt pretty. The Spice Girls spoke about embracing your flaws, and the importance of relationships, which were reflected in their lyrics about the importance of putting friends before lovers and celebrating your mum.

The message proved to be overwhelmingly powerful to pre-teen and teen girls. As the Spice Girls brand exploded into films and merchandise, brands rushed to monetize girl power, and targeted the emerging tweeny market, which despite the attempts of the previous waves of the women's movement, was still awash with pink plastic, princess costumes and impossibly-breasted Barbies. A new generation of women were growing up with the mainstream idea that girls could do anything, and by 2010 this ripple effect would herald in the fourth wave.

Opposite: Lil' Kim on her No Way Out tour, 1997. With her explicit songs about female sexuality and self-love, Kim brought honesty to 1990s rap.

VAGINA,
I'M TALKING TO YOU
WOMEN'S BODIES IN
THE SPOTLIGHT

The decade of power brought a new awareness to the female experience. For some, this centred around the body, while for others, the 1990s signalled the opportunity for a new exploration of the mind.

New play *The Vagina Monologues* brought women together to talk about one important thing: how they felt about their bodies. This was the decade that had ushered in the supermodel and perpetuated sexist stereotypes in music videos, but it had also brought women's stories, in the form of the confessional, into the spotlight.

Released in 1993, Susanna Kaysen's bestselling memoir *Girl, Interrupted* detailed her stay in a mental institution, and was made into the 1999 film of the same name starring Winona Ryder and Angelina Jolie. Kathryn Harrison's controversial 1997 memoir, *The Kiss*, detailed the author's affair with her biological father. And then there was Elizabeth Wurtzel's *Prozac Nation*, which broke new ground in the way it unashamedly dealt, in a frank, new way, with the effects of female depression, and the inner sanctum of both the female brain and body, through the prism of self-harming,

Opposite: Eve Ensler in 1999 performing her hit play *The Vagina Monologues*, an episodic piece about women's relationship with their bodies.

overdosing and one-night stands. These books, particularly Wurtzel's, which was published when the author was 27 and made her into a Gen X touchstone, would spur the confessional memoir trend, which continues to this day.

In the wake of this wave of introspection, *The Vagina Monologues* went further. It grappled with gender politics, female identity, body shaming and sexuality – and most importantly the thing at the heart of it all: what it meant to be a woman. Written by native

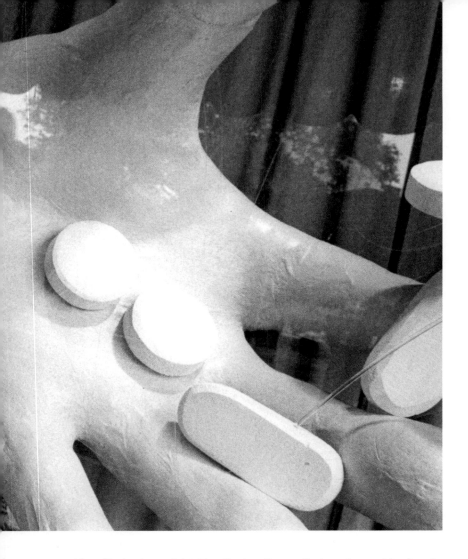

New York playwright Eve Ensler, it was first performed by her in 1996 in a Greenwich Village café basement. Presented as an hour-long, one-woman show, Ensler narrated a series of monologues fictionalized from the accounts of real women she had interviewed. These were narratives of the most intimate and honest kind – they

Above: Elizabeth Wurtzel's introspective memoir *Prozac Nation* launched a wave of books about what it meant to be a Gen-X woman.

dealt with periods, pubic hair, sexual experiences, abuse, rape, genital mutilation and relationships, as well as giving name to the exact way women felt about their vaginas, in multisensory, technicolour language. The play's groundbreaking and raw portrayal on stage shone a spotlight on the power of women's lived experience and testimony. And it was praised for its warm humorous tone, being authentic, funny and poignant in turn, as well as being an important piece of feminist art that provoked important conversations around the very thing that most women had been trained not to even speak of in public. Women flocked to see *The Vagina Monologues*, harking back to the consciousness-raising groups of the 1970s, when women had come together to share their truths.

By February 14, 1998, the play had reached such stellar heights that celebrities including Winona Ryder, Glenn Close, Whoopi Goldberg and Susan Sarandon were performing it as part of a benefit to raise money for domestic violence charities. That "V-Day" performance was such a hit, Ensler was inspired to make the occasion a permanent fixture.

More than 20 years on, *The Vagina Monologues* has been translated into 48 languages and performed in more than 140 countries. In the early 2000s, Ensler responded to criticism that her play excluded transgender perspectives by including material created from interviews with transgender women.

Above: In 1999, actresses including Cate Blanchett, Thandiwe Newton, Kate Winslet and Melanie Griffith donned red boas for the annual V-Day Vagina Monologues benefit.

THE PROBLEM PAGE
MAGAZINES THAT MATTERED

From Riot grrrl fanzines to monthly glossies with a bold, empowering viewpoint, the 1990s was the golden age of exciting and intelligent women's magazines with distinctly feminist perspectives.

Remember when everyone read women's magazines? It's hard to envision from our vantage point of the 2020s, when – despite a 90s-retro-inspired resurgence of fanzines and the existence of the wondrous gal-dem.com – quality women's publications are thin on the ground. But in the 1990s magazines were everything. Packed with advice and information for women of all ages, from teenagers getting their periods to young women in relationships or embarking on careers, to new mothers having babies – there was a time when women's weeklies and glossies were essential.

Ever since the 1970s, when feminists strove to disseminate their messages, feminism had become inextricably intertwined with magazines. In 1990 Naomi Wolf, writing in *The Beauty Myth*, saw magazines as the medium that had popularized feminist ideas more widely than any other, making them accessible to all strata of society. Women's magazines, she argued, were "very potent instruments of social change", as well as tools which engendered female solidarity.

First there were zines. The Riot grrrl bands of the early part of the decade had taken their cues from the punk movement and

Opposite: *Emma*, August 1995. Launched in 1977 by Alice Schwarzer, *Emma* is still Germany's leading feminist magazine. The tagline translates as "The magazine by women for humans".

EMMA

DAS MAGAZIN VON FRAUEN FÜR MENSCHEN

11,80/Nr. 4
G 4155 F
Juli/Aug. 95

11,80 DM 11,80 SFr 95 ÖS

TANK GIRL
Emanze oder Tussi?

Schimmel
Friedenspreis für
Fundamentalistin?

Lesbengewalt
Auch Frauen
schlagen Frauen

FOTOPREIS: DIE SIEGERINNEN!

Sassy

APRIL '92

ain't love
grand?
KURT
OF NIRVANA AND
COURTNEY
OF HOLE

A DAY IN THE LIFE OF
**miss
america,**
INDENTURED SERVANT

Above: *Sassy* magazine, April 1992. The Kurt and Courtney feature inside praised the Nirvana frontman for being in love with an "opinionated, feminist, ambitious rocker".

Opposite: Issue 1 of Molly Neuman and Allison Wolfe's *Riot Grrrl* zine, which was handed out at gigs and posted to subscribers, spreading the word of the movement beyond the music.

combined music-making with the creation of fanzines. These low-fi, handmade affairs were handwritten, or typed on typewriters or computers, stuck together and photocopied, illustrated with felt-tip doodles, pencil drawings and cut-up pictures collaged from comics and catalogues. Zines commented on the shallowness of women's media and depictions of women in the press, as at the same time they gave information about festivals and told stories about women's lives.

Mainly in the US, where reader numbers could support a wider variety of "niche" titles, the explosion of zines was the precursor to offbeat women's publications that provided an alternative to the relationship advice and fashion spreads of *Cosmo* and *Vogue*.

Launched in 1988, America's *Sassy* was ostentatiously feminist, with cover stories on how to be a girl drummer, growing armpit hair, travelling the world, standing up for yourself, fighting back against street harassment, raising feminist children and even recipes by Sonic Youth's Kim Gordon. In 1993 came the founding of another defiantly feminist title, *Bust* (its tagline was "For women with something to get off their chests"). It began life as a stapled zine and grew to a glossy, presenting articles on pop culture, fashion and beauty through the lens of its intelligent feminist editors. *Bitch*, founded in 1996, took a slightly less shiny, more serious route (it touted itself as "a feminist response to pop culture"), with an approach which critiqued and questioned contemporary culture and explored women's issues. (*Bitch* and *Bust* are both still going, having diversified with the times.)

Wagadon, publishers of *The Face* and *Arena*, launched *Frank* in 1997. While not overtly feminist in its politics, it attempted to give women more rounded fare than most of the glossies, with features about current affairs and politics, fashion spreads featuring pregnant women and a sex-positive attitude.

Some time in the mid-2000s, magazines dwindled in number and declined in quality, as the inception of the Internet reduced concentration spans and the need for printed material. At the same time, increasing competition for ad revenue impelled publishers to abandon challenging ideas and forward-thinking editorials, and push toward blander, advertiser-friendly, product-promoting "content". But in the 1990s that all seemed a very long way off.

Opposite: From 1977 to 1992, Britain's *Shocking Pink* was run by a series of collectives and aimed at teenagers and young women.

WHY LUKE PERRY'S NAME MAKES YOU WANT TO BUY THIS
sassyscans.tumblr.com

Sassy

37 ways to blow a relationship ACCORDING TO A GUY

reforming teenage murderers— SHOULD WE BOTHER?

DO YOU need armpit hair to be a feminist? THE SASSY DEBATE

90210 BACKLASH AND MORE ENTERTAINMENT POLL SHOCKERS

Sassy

IT'S HER! THE NEW **SASSIEST GIRL** IN AMERICA

LISA, 16, GOES HOME AFTER THE **FLOOD**

WHAT TO DO WHEN YOUR **FRIENDSHIP** ROTS

FRILLY CLOTHES THAT AREN'T PRISSY

sassyscans.tumblr.com

È tutta nuova. noidonne

No, a casa non ci torno
Con le donne di Sarajevo
Irigaray: l'Abc dell'amore

MARZO 1993

noidonne

nervosa?

Mimosa!

These pages: 1990s issues of America's *Sassy* magazine, Italy's longstanding *Noi Donne* and the UK's short-lived *Frank*. All were mainstream glossies exploring feminist themes.

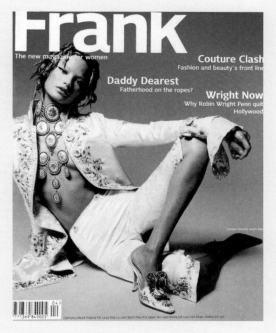

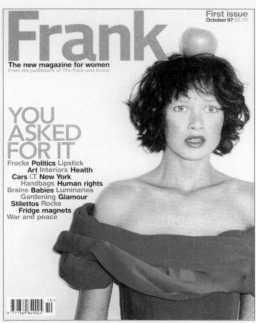

WOMEN KICK OFF
HEROINES OF FEMALE FOOTBALL

A highpoint for the women's game, in the 1990s women's football finally came to prominence. Some important events and high-profile athletes both helped to launch and launched a new female-fronted sporting landscape.

In 1999, the Women's World Cup Final, China v USA, took place on a hot July afternoon in California. After regular and extra time, the match was being decided in a penalty shootout. Brandi Chastain, already a women's soccer star for the USA, stepped up to take her shot. The tension mounted, not least for Chastain herself. There were 90,000 people in the stands, a global TV audience of close to 400 million (40 million of whom were US viewers) – all of which were records for a women's team sporting event. As the crowd held its breath, Chastain scored. In celebration, she ripped off her top and dropped to her knees. The photograph of Chastain in her sports bra, grinning, her fists raised in triumph went around the world. Twenty years on, the image – at once joyful, defiant and subversive – remains the most iconic image in the history of women's sports.

Chastain's celebration punctuated a pivotal decade that was to put women's football on the map. For decades women had made successful careers of individual sports including tennis, golf and Olympic events, creating female sports superstars such as tennis's

Opposite: The iconic bra-tastic photo of the USA's Brandi Chastain, celebrating her winning penalty kick at the 1999 Women's World Cup final.

Billie Jean King and Martina Navratilova, track star Wilma Rudolph and German skater Katerina Witt. Women's team sports, and football in particular, however, had been relegated to amateur status, despite a long history that went back to the First World War.

The 1990s were different. The first two Women's Football World Cups – China '91 and Sweden '95 – had drawn fans in, but USA '99 was on another level. The resulting spotlight shone on the women's game in general, and soaring TV viewership figures attracted the attention of sponsors such as Nike, undoubtedly lured by the 30 million women and girls participating in the sport across the globe by the middle of the decade. By the 1999 World Cup, women's football had become so mainstream that Mattel brought out a World Cup Barbie. The result was in an instant pay rise for players in some of the biggest women's leagues, including Germany's Frauen-Bundesliga, Sweden's Damallsvenskan and Japan's Nadeshiko League.

In Germany, the football association had long deemed women too frail to play organized football, finally relenting in the 1970s, only with new rules that demanded a lighter ball, forbade the wearing of studded boots, and reduced the length of matches to 20 minutes less than the men's game. But then in 1989, at the European Competition for Women's Football, Germany's Die Nationalelf beat Norway in a zingy final that drew 23,000 spectators and a huge TV audience (the first live women's match ever to be broadcast in the country). This was when the Frauen-Bundesliga was born.

In the two decades since Chastain's celebration, there have been ups and downs. America's Women's United Soccer League folded in 2003, prompting FIFA's then-president Sepp Blatter to say that it might be time to sex up the women's game with "more feminine uniforms, perhaps tighter shorts". In 2018 Norway's Ada Hegerberg became the inaugural winner of FIFA's Ballon d'Or Féminin, a seminal

Opposite: Team USA celebrating their victory after defeating Canada 5–0 at the 1991 CONCACAF Women's Soccer Championships in Haiti.

moment for the game that was marred by the ceremony's French host asking her if she would twerk to celebrate.

Professional women footballers remain undervalued and underpaid: while players in the English Women's Super League, one of the richest female competitions, can earn up to £200,000 (though that is rare), salaries start at £20,000; the average salary in the English Premier League in 2021 was £3m. On the eve of the Women's World Cup in France in 2019, the players of the USA national team sued the US Soccer Federation, demanding the same compensation as their male counterparts. It was also revealed the FIFA prize money on offer was $30 million for women and $400 million for men. France '19 saw a record one billion viewers across 206 countries, and more than one million tickets sold. When the USA were awarded their trophy after beating the Netherlands in the final, the crowd chanted "equal pay" and booed FIFA president Gianni Infantino. FIFA has promised to double the prize money in the next World Cup. But when it comes to equality in sport, there is still very much a need for women to kick off.

Right: Team USA jubilantly hoist the World Cup after beating Norway 2–1 in 1991.

Overleaf: Nigeria's Oyeka Anna Agumanu and Omon-Love Branch take on Germany's Heidi Mohr at the very first FIFA Women's World Cup in 1991, 61 years after the men's first World Cup in 1930.

2000s–present

BLOODY SHAME
THE RISE OF PERIOD PRIDE

With some key battles behind them, in the 2000s, feminists could move onto celebrating menstruation and finding ways to eliminate period shame and stigma through art, activism and product design.

The new millennium saw feminists turning their focus toward the natural bodily function that had been denigrated as "the curse" and portrayed in advertising as something that needed to be hidden away: menstrual periods. Now placing it at the centre of conversations around sex positivity, body positivity and equality in feminism, the feminists of the 2000s began to recognize that while the onset of menstruation defined womanhood, it simultaneously othered women and made them feel ashamed, embarrassed, even afraid, of their own bodies. That needed to change.

Periods were brought into the open with a new raft of consciousness-raising initiatives for young girls, like "period kits" and other products created by female-led start-up companies such as Seattle's Dot Girl. In 2006 their First Period Kit launched, which included pads, an information booklet, a menstrual calendar, and a heat pack for cramps. Other kits soon followed suit, which intended to celebrate and destigmatize the first-period experience.

This decade saw sanitary protection brands move on from the era of the euphemistic "Woah Bodyform!" adverts – with menstruating

Opposite: In 2015 Kiran Gandhi drew attention from around the world when she ran the London Marathon while free-bleeding to de-stigmatize menstruation. Here she is with friends at the finish line.

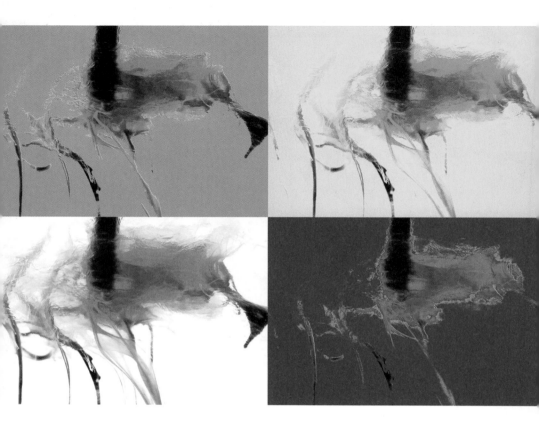

women joyfully jumping out of planes, riding horses and roller-skating – towards more realistic, even funny campaigns. Always announced in 2005 that it was "reframing" periods as a positive experience with a light-hearted campaign about having a "happy period". Kotex made waves in Australia in 2008, with a TV advert showing a woman and her friendly animated beaver (tagline: "You've only got one..."). In 2009 Tampax launched a campaign of humorous adverts showing "Mother Nature" giving women an unwanted gift.

Concerns around the environment, as well as this destigmatizing, led to the launch of eco-friendly, more "hands-on" menstrual products in this decade, such as reusable silicone menstrual cups. The Mooncup, launched in 2002, and the DivaCup, launched in 2003, both offered practical and environmental advantages to tampons, and would slowly increase in popularity as a new generation of women grew up.

With periods in the collective consciousness, the 2000s saw attention directed to concerns around equality: namely, the so-called tampon tax. In many countries, essential sanitary protection for women was subject to a mark-up in the form of sales tax, classifying the products as luxury goods. This, feminists argued, specifically punished women economically for their normal bodily functions. In 2000 the tax on tampons in the UK was reduced to 5 per cent and finally abolished after 20 years of campaigning in 2020. In 2004 Kenya was the first country to abolish it entirely, and the late 2010s saw a big move globally toward widespread tampon tax elimination.

In 2017 it was widely reported in several countries around the developed world, including Britain, France and the US, that young women and girls were staying home from school or having to be provided with sanitary wear by teachers because of widespread "period poverty". In parts of the developing world the issue remains

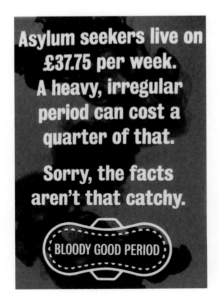

Opposite: US feminist artist Jen Lewis makes artwork from her menstrual blood. This piece is called *Truth & Perception.*

Left: Sign held by Bloody Good Period activists at the 2019 Women's March.

extreme, with Action Aid reporting that 1 in 10 African girls misses school regularly because of periods, and that 12 per cent of India's menstruating women (about 43 million people) can't afford sanitary products. Governments are reacting to this, if slowly – in 2019 Scotland became the first country to make sanitary products freely available in schools, universities and colleges.

Menstrual activists began to emerge toward the end of the decade, with the aim of normalizing periods as well as highlighting the issues faced by menstruating women. In 2014 Kiran Gandhi ran the London Marathon while "freebleeding", to highlight period destigmatization. The same year the underwear brand Thinx used a high-profile campaign to advertise their period knickers on the New York subway – and followed that up in 2018 with a study that said that 58 per cent of US women have felt embarrassed for being on their period. In France, period activism is a growing phenomenon, with spaces such as Cyclique, a website dedicated to menstruation information and gynaecological health set up by menstrual activist Fanny Godebarge.

Opposite: Bloody laundry at a 2019 period pride rally, photographed by Elainea Emmott.

Above: UK charity Bloody Good Period provide sanitary protection for asylum seekers and refugees, working to eradicate the shame and stigma surrounding periods.

HIBO WARDERE

ACTIVIST & EDUCATOR

ON BEING AN FGM ACTIVIST

I'm from a community in Somalia where almost 97 per cent of girls and women have been – and are still being – cut and mutilated. In Somalia they perform the cruellest of all types of female genital mutilation (FGM). There are levels of severity, and the one I had, they rip everything off and you're left with nothing resembling genitalia. Your labia aren't there, your clitoris isn't there and then they stitch you up and leave you with a tiny hole out of which you can hardly pee. You can't have periods, have sex, have kids. I was like that when I arrived in the UK in 1989 aged 18. The first thing I did was seek medical help. I was opened up – it's called de-infibulation – and that's when life began for me. I married an amazing man who was there when I wanted to cry. But I still didn't know how to address the pain and psychological anguish.

Eleven years ago I was working in a primary school and there was a suspected case of FGM. I decided to write an essay about me, and give it to the headteacher. It was in broken English – and raging with anger – but it turned out to be the start of something bigger. I began speaking to my colleagues at school. I found my voice. I was angry and I wanted the world to know what I and what many others had gone through.

In Somalia, FGM has been part of life for 3,000 years. If you aren't cut, you are seen as unclean and impure – you can't make a good marriage. Mothers see it as protection for their daughters. Who are they causing the lifelong damage – sometimes death – for? It's so the future husband can have a woman who's never going to cheat, as her sex drive is very low, who is going to be easy to control in every sense. FGM causes infertility. And when you do have a child, the maternal death rate is staggering. Your sexual feelings are disrupted. Your human right to enjoy your body is denied.

I travel around the globe talking to policy makers. I want everyone to see this is isn't a black thing, or an Asian thing, or a Muslim thing – it's a human rights issue. In the UK I train professionals from doctors and teachers to community workers. The work I adore is teaching our young people. Education is key; knowledge is freedom. I think we will see FGM end within a generation if we continue with education. I want to speak for the girls that are still mutilated around the globe. I owe it to them to be talking as long as I have breath left.

SHE WORE JEANS
FEMINISM AND ASSAULT

The era when rape and domestic violence laws around the world came into focus, the 2000s saw a wave of feminist campaigning and protests take place all over the world.

The issues of rape and sexual assault have always been important to the modern women's movement. In the context of the oppressive patriarchy, rape culture was part of the pervading culture that not only encouraged male supremacy, but also stigmatized, slut-shamed and blamed the victim. From the consciousness-raising groups of the 1970s, women have fought to destigmatize the "shame" of rape victims, as well as push for harsher laws to punish perpetrators of sexual violence against women. In the late twentieth century, rape culture seemed to be as present as ever, with the sexualization of media and the rise of porn and porn culture.

As the 1990s turned into the 2000s, jeans – once a symbol of women's sartorial freedom – became representative of something completely different. When it came to sexual violence against women, Italy had been one of the countries that was resistant to change. Up until 1996, rape was defined as a crime against public morality and decency, rather than a crime of violence perpetrated against a victim that highlighted body autonomy. Furthermore, until 1981, if a rapist married his victim (including if she was a minor), the rape would no longer be classed as

Opposite: Columbia University student Emma Sulkowicz in 2014, protesting the lack of action after she was raped on campus. *Mattress Performance (Carry That Weight)* doubled as her visual arts degree thesis.

an offence in law. A new reform bill in 1996, written by 67 female members of Italy's parliament, reclassified rape as a criminal felony. In 1998 this progress was rewound when a 1992 conviction for rape was overturned on the grounds that the 18-year-old victim had been wearing tight jeans, and therefore must have allowed her rapist to remove them; it was argued that this demonstrated the victim had not fought her attacker hard enough. In response to the overturning, Italy's women politicians started wearing jeans to parliament in protest. In 1999 the first "Denim Day" was held and continues to be an annual protest event against erroneous and destructive attitudes toward sexual harassment, abuse, assault and rape.

In Spain in 2018, the outcome of the "wolf pack" case provoked one of the biggest ever feminist uprisings in the country's history. During

the running of the bulls in Pamplona in 2016, five men had carried out the gang rape of an 18-year-old woman, but were acquitted and found guilty of the lesser crime of sexual violence – because the law only defined rape as occurring with coercive violence. In protest, hundreds of thousands of women all over Spain took to the streets, holding signs that read "*Yo te creo*" (I believe you), in what has since been called the country's biggest ever feminist protest and has created a seismic shift in active feminism in Spain. There have since been multiple protests relating to the case, including public protests held on

Above: In 1999, deputies Stefania Prestigiacomo, Alessandra Mussolini and Sandra Fei protest the Italian courts ruling that a woman in jeans could not have been raped.

International Women's Day, calling for a change in the law. In 2019 Spain's Supreme Court overturned the verdict and changed it to one of rape, increasing the attackers' prison sentences to 15 years. In 2021 Spain approved a bill defining all non-consensual sex as rape, joining other European countries including Sweden (who was first to remove the definition of rape as taking place within a threatening or violent context, and first to introduce a consent-based law). Other countries who have since reformed their rape laws include Denmark, Greece, Iceland and The Netherlands. To date, many other countries around the world still define rape wholly within the context of violence.

Above: Susan Brownmiller published *Against Our Will: Men, Women and Rape* in 1975, which groundbreakingly defined rape as a political problem and feminist issue, rather than an individual crime.

Opposite: Madrid women protest against the release of the "wolf pack" on bail in 2018. The wave of protests around the country kick-started a new era of feminism for young Spanish women.

HARRIET WISTRICH

DIRECTOR & FOUNDER, CENTRE
FOR WOMEN'S JUSTICE

ON COMBATTING VIOLENCE
AGAINST WOMEN

I have always been passionate about feminism and an activist from when I first met like-minded others. We campaigned around women's right to abortion, negative representation in the media, and challenging all forms of violence against women. In the early 1990s, I co-founded Justice for Women, to highlight the discrimination women faced in the criminal justice system and specifically to challenge the murder convictions of women driven to kill violent and abusive partners. We organized protests outside the Royal Courts of Justice in support of the appeals of Sara Thornton and Kiranjit Ahluwalia, highlighting the sexist defence of provocation that was available to men who exploded in rage and killed their wives but not to women subject to the "slower burn" provocation of the abusive, controlling and violent behaviour of their husbands.

In 1992 Emma Humphreys, a young woman already seven years into a life sentence, wrote to us from prison requesting our help. She had suffered multiple forms of male violence from childhood, culminating in her entry into street prostitution in Nottingham, aged just 16. There she met a man who controlled and abused her until, prior to one more rape, she took a kitchen knife and stabbed him fatally. The shame and degradation of the violence she was subjected to meant that when faced with only men prosecuting, defending and trying her at trial, she was silent and could not speak in her own defence. I volunteered to obtain her life story and helped a new legal team build grounds of appeal. Working on her case persuaded me to train as a lawyer and I completed my studies, aged 35, just days before Emma's successful appeal.

I had found a vocation where I could combine my passion for feminism with achieving change for women. Twenty years later I formed the Centre for Women's Justice, a legal charity aimed at holding the state to account around violence against women and girls.

DOMESTIC
GODDESSES
SUBVERSIVE CRAFTING

Embracing traditionally domestic arts, the women of the 2000s found new creative ways to use knitting, crochet and cross stitch as acts of feminist artistic expression, political protest and general, joyful defiance.

I n the UK, the Women's Institute (WI) had been formed during the First World War as a way of uniting women – especially those in far-flung rural communities. By the time the 2000s dawned, the WI was considered a relic of the past, where little old ladies baked cakes and knitted booties in village halls. That was soon to change, with a new trend for all things nostalgic.

This was the decade in which vintage fashion exploded – no doubt aided by eBay going public in 1998 and the launch, in 2005, of handicraft–slash–vintage emporium Etsy, as well as the counter-culture's reaction to the stratospheric rise of fast fashion. Crafters were turning their skills into successful businesses, with craft markets, workshops and pop-ups appearing across the globe, from community centres to luxury stores. Decades from the 1940s to the 1980s were being referenced in style and the media. Young women were listening to retro-tinged music such as electroclash, learning to lindy hop at club nights, becoming burlesque dancers, crafting, baking cupcakes – and joining the WI. The Shoreditch Sisters was a WI chapter launched in 2007 by Joe Strummer's craft-loving daughter Jazz Domino Holly, located in a hip area of London, with millennial members mostly in their twenties. More importantly, the Sisters were

Above: Rachael Matthews, founder of Cast Off Knitting Club and the Prick Your Finger art space. Matthews continues to make textile art.

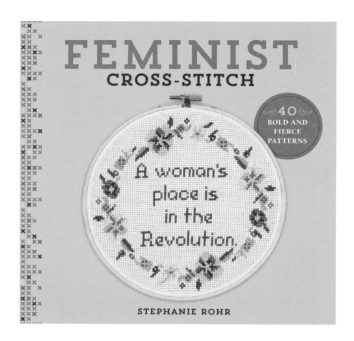

political and attended marches such as SlutWalk and Million Women Rise. The Sisters were as much about reclaiming the traditional female pursuits of baking and sewing as exchanging political ideas and campaigning for change. The young, new wave of the WI took hold, with groups being created all over Britain.

"Stitch and bitch" groups, which had originated in the US in the 1940s as a variant of the WI, were similarly reclaimed in the 2000s by feminists such as *Bust* magazine's Debbie Stoller in New York City and in London by textile artist Rachael Matthews (whose group, founded in 2000, was called Cast Off). The noughties' stitch-and-bitch sessions took place in pubs and cafés, in art galleries and on the Tube, making what were formerly women's private domestic tasks a public event. Instead of making socks for their husbands, the stitch-and-bitchers of the 2000s had political discussions and a punk rock spirit; they were creating art pieces, using alternative materials and making political statements – sewing cross-stitch with feminist messages and embroidering vagina quilts. The craftivist movement encouraged a new, gentle form of activism, in which women came together to create messages of protest. The Craftivist Collective, a group led by campaigner Sarah Corbett, held "stitch-ins" that recalled the consciousness-raising groups of the 1970s, where women could discuss political issues, while using "craft as a tool for change".

With their retro activities, women in the 2000s had reclaimed femininity and used it as a badge of pride. Some saw this as a backwards step, which succumbed to the stereotypes of the patriarchy and was indistinguishable from stereotypes. But the generation of young women who found it empowering would be the next decade's leaders and tastemakers. The millennials were coming.

Opposite: Cross stitch artist Stephanie Rohr uses the traditionally female art to protest feminist issues, stitching slogans including "Smash the patriarchy" and "Nasty woman"

Below: Women at Knitty City, New York, 2017. Handmade knitted "pussyhats" became the popular symbol of female Trump-resistance during the Women's March protests following his election.

PERSONAL TESTIMONY

LAURA PERLONGO

TV HOST & PRODUCER

ON MILLENNIAL FEMINISM AND MOTHERHOOD

When I was in my twenties, I would look at pregnant women and think, "*Why* did she let him do that to her?" I thought the bump was a bad look. It represented giving up, giving in, proving them right. Proving a woman would likely never become a prolific artist or scientist or CEO of something very big and important. I was a FEMINIST!

The problem was, my version of feminism didn't allow for diverse expressions of the female experience. My version of feminism then went along with the idea that money and prestige is worth more than motherhood. Worth more than the *currently* unpaid work of building families and community. Worth more than love itself.

Now in my thirties, with three children, I very much would like to sit that near-sighted 20-year-old wannabe feminist down and shake her out of whatever 1980s sitcom coma had her tripping for a decade. In feminism, "equal" cannot mean "same". We are not equal until we can all explore every part of this world and ourselves without judgement. We are not equal until we are all afforded the freedom to be different. To make unique choices about who we are and want to be that are built into our economy so that little girls don't see pregnant women as the enemy to their capitalist dreams. Maybe they will even be allowed and afforded dreams that include a pregnancy. Gasp! *Maybe* they won't even rush back to work! GASP! GASP!

When I was pregnant I wore that bump out. Crop-tops, open jackets, late nights. I didn't hide myself or my babies postpartum either. To this day I bring them on planes, in offices and to dinner. Doesn't matter where. They're a welcome part of my life as a feminist. Kinda my favourite part, if I'm really being honest.

BIG LOVE
BODY POSITIVITY AND FEMINISM

The buzzwords of the 2010s, body positivity and diversity, became important issues for millennial feminists, with fashion brands and the media taking up the baton and celebrating women of all sizes and shapes.

As the decades of the twentieth century rolled over into the twenty-first, so too did the ideals around women's body shapes. In 1978 Susie Orbach had declared "fat is a feminist issue". Unattainable representations of women's bodies were tied to feminism because they repressed women and held them to different standards than men. It was mostly women who suffered from eating disorders, were criticized based on weight and sexual attractiveness, and were objectified by their physical appearance.

The highly sexualized landscape of the late 1990s and early 2000s had seen the rise of porn culture and uber-sexualized celebrities who often had exaggerated plastic surgery. Magazines and film had perfected digital airbrushing, leading to distorted images of celebrities who embodied physical "perfection". Fashion had swung from the high glamour of the impossibly beautiful supermodel to the grungy waif look embodied by Kate Moss and known as "heroin chic". Extremely skinny women headed up TV shows such as *Ally McBeal* and *Sex and the City*. Thinness as a body ideal for women was in vogue.

Opposite: Lizzo performing at the 2019 American Music Awards. In the 2010s the singer became celebrated as a body positivity and self-love icon.

Step forward the size-acceptance movement. The movement's ideas – that people should not be discriminated against because of size, and that women should learn to love rather than hate their bodies – were not new (especially in the USA, where the National Association to Advance Fat Acceptance had been launched in 1969). But these ideas had especially gathered momentum in the 1990s as the zine movement and Riot grrrl engendered fat liberation zines. In 1997 two women launched the non-profit organization they called The Body Positive. Connie Sobczak and Elizabeth Scott had both felt the harmful effects of eating disorders – Sobczak losing her sister to the disease and suffering from the affliction herself, and Scott as a psychotherapist turned social worker who had become overwhelmed by the suffering she witnessed in her young female clients. They wanted to help women who suffered from body issues and eating disorders. An inclusive, supportive platform was launched, which is still in place today.

By the 2000s fat feminism had entered the public consciousness. The Internet blogosphere had taken over from zines as a way for fat feminists to come together and share ideas. Websites like PeopleofSize.com, The Fat Chick and Marilyn Wann's Fat!So? (which had started out as a 1990s zine) sprung up, as well as individual blogs run by women campaigning for body positivity and fat visibility, fostering support and community around size-acceptance issues.

The 2010s have seen the Internet take fat feminism further, with a marked swing towards representation of differently sized women's bodies, aided by the cultural shift towards more feminist viewpoints, as well as the launch of social media platforms that enabled widespread image-sharing. Plus-size beauty icons are highly visible and being used in advertising and fashion campaigns

Opposite: Intimates label Aerie has become known for its body positive, all-age, diverse stance. Here are the brand's "Role Models" at an event in 2020.

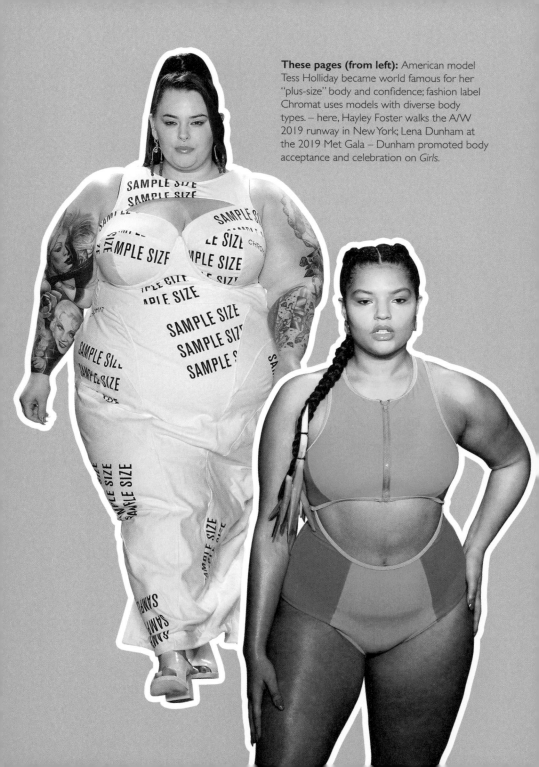

These pages (from left): American model Tess Holliday became world famous for her "plus-size" body and confidence; fashion label Chromat uses models with diverse body types. – here, Hayley Foster walks the A/W 2019 runway in New York; Lena Dunham at the 2019 Met Gala – Dunham promoted body acceptance and celebration on *Girls*.

as brands seek to reflect the shift toward diverse and inclusive authenticity. Influencers like Megan Jayne Crabbe and Stephanie Yeboah are leading the curve, along with models such as Tess Holliday and Ashley Graham, who made headlines in 2019 when she posted an Instagram image of her natural naked body featuring stretch marks and flesh rolls. When the Aerie underwear brand launched in 2014, it was with a promise that they would use models of diverse size and shape, and not digitally alter them. The brand also became the first to sponsor the US National Eating Disorders Association. In 2018 actor Jameela Jamil launched her Instagram and website i-weigh, which aims to promote body acceptance, diversity and change through "radical inclusion". The future looks bright – and body positive.

Right: 2019's *Booksmart*, directed by Olivia Wilde and starring Beanie Feldstein and Kaitlyn Dever, feels emblematic of the change in the movie industry post #MeToo.

I'M WITH HER

THE MARCH THAT SHOOK
THE WORLD

Creating a seismic global moment, the first Women's March was a
historic day when women came together on an unprecedented scale
to make their voices heard and speak truth to power.

January 21, 2017, was the day of Donald Trump's presidential
inauguration. Throughout his campaign Trump had signalled
his intentions to institute a conservative, far-right administration
that would seek to actively roll back women's rights. Alongside this,
reports were continually surfacing which evidenced the would-be
president's historical misogynistic, derogatory, abusive behaviour
and attitude towards women. There was a sense among feminists
that Trump's election would have disastrous effects for women in
America and around the world.

It was a retired lawyer, Hawaii-based Teresa Shook, who first
posited the idea of a response in the form of a women's protest march
and created a Facebook event; in New York, fashion designer Bob
Bland did the same. The idea quickly gained traction through social
media, with thousands voicing support for a DC "Women's March"
as it came to be known, including women around the world who
began to plan simultaneous supportive demonstrations in their own

Opposite and overleaf: The Women's March on January 21, 2017, was a
triumphant moment for women – an estimated 500,000 people came to
Washington DC to protest Trump's inauguration and right-wing, anti-feminist
policies. Many donned pink pussyhats and held homemade signs, sending a
powerful message to the new administration.

countries. None of them could have known that they were making history – and that more than 670 women's marches would be held across seven continents, with an estimated 6 million people taking part globally.

In Washington DC, at the original march, 500,000 people converged – thought to be around double the number that turned out for the inauguration itself. They were young and old, men and women together, pushing buggies, holding the hands of their children, wearing knitted pink "pussyhats", flowers and pink clothing. High-profile figures who marched included Gloria Steinem, Angela Davis, Madonna, Rihanna and Yoko Ono, making rallying speeches or performing specially written songs. The marchers shouted, sang and carried rainbow flags and homemade signs that read "Hands off

my pussy!", "Love trumps hate" and "Keep your tiny hands off our rights!". New York City saw 400,000 marching, Los Angeles upward of 500,000, London had 100,000 people and Toronto 60,000, with other large-scale protests happening in Paris, Frankfurt, Brussels, Copenhagen, Geneva, Oslo, Stockholm, Sydney, Auckland and Montreal, and in countries including Kenya, North Korea, Japan, Israel and India. It was, everyone agreed, a historic day for women.

Since the days of the suffragettes, supporters of the women's movement had been coming together to protest publicly. The women's lib marches of the 1960s and 1970s had seen large numbers of women protesting equality and civil rights, resulting in thousands of

Below: In Brussels, women held "Lights for rights" during the 2017 Women's March.

women orchestrating attention-grabbing demonstrations, organizing marches and staging sit-ins. Starting in 1989, America had seen an incredible rising-up of people, demonstrating in support of enhanced pro-choice legislation (the 1989 March for Women's Lives had 600,000 protesters; the 1992 edition of the same march had 750,000, while the 2004 edition had a record 1.15 million). But the 2017 Women's March was something on a different scale. The age of the Internet ushered in with it the powerful ability for women of all generations to share information and ideas. The SlutWalks of the early 2010s – which began as a Toronto demonstration protesting an incident of a rape victim being blamed by a police officer, and soon became a huge global street protest event – had been the first sign that the new generation of feminists were not going to take infractions of their freedoms lying down. The Women's March of 2017 cemented it.

The Women's March is now regarded as the largest single-day women's demonstration in world history. The sheer size and cultural impact of the Women's March cannot be underestimated, despite the fact that, like many other forms of feminist activity, it has since been criticized for its lack of diversity and general elitism. It mobilized women on a truly enormous scale, representing for many the first time they had taken part in a political demonstration. That it had happened at all made many women feel a glimmer of optimism about their power to create change and about the mass-awareness of feminism and women's politics it indicated, despite the global rise of right-wing politics. The media was suddenly awash with discussions about feminism. The fourth wave, many declared, had finally arrived.

Opposite: (top left) In Santa Fe, New Mexico, Native American protesters used the 2019 Women's March to critique the treatment of indigenous women in the USA; (top right) the 2017 Women's March in Paris, with the Eiffel Tower in the background; (centre) Belgrade's 2017 Women's March featured a banner saying "Women's March against fascism"; (bottom) in Amsterdam on January 21, 2017, thousands demonstrated outside the American consulate.

PERSONAL TESTIMONY

NADIA GHULAM

WRITER & CAMPAIGNER

ON THE POWER OF
EDUCATION FOR GIRLS

I grew up in Kabul during the Afghanistan War. When I was eight years old, a bomb fell on our house and I was seriously injured. I spent two years in hospital.

The Taliban were saying women could not go out, study or work. My father was a pharmacist but he became crazy with post-traumatic stress. Aged 11, I decided to disguise myself as a man so I could earn money, so my family could eat. I went to work in construction, digging wells. In the beginning it wasn't difficult as I had a lot of facial injuries and wore a turban. It was harder as I started puberty, but I had tricks so they wouldn't discover me – I didn't eat for six months. I got very skinny so I wouldn't have breasts or look physically like a woman. I ended up dressing as a man for 10 years. I was afraid 24 hours a day, every second of my life. Even now when I am far away and somewhere safe, I am still living that fear.

I came to Spain with the help of a non-profit organization. When a Spanish journalist wanted an interview, I asked to be paid with a course of English classes. Then I worked as her translator – dressed as a man, I could take her to places she couldn't go alone. She took me to Spain – I was 21 when I got here. A Catalan family took me in and got me an education. I am now doing a master's degree in international development.

Education has given me my independence, my autonomy. In Afghanistan, they say God tells women not to study, and women accept it because they don't have enough knowledge. A woman's freedom is decided by her husband, her brother, her relative. Women can't earn their own money or live alone. When I wore men's clothes, I saw myself as equal to them. It made me happy that I earned the same salary as men. They were amazed by my strength and didn't know I was a girl.

Three things have helped me in my life: my mother, my education and fate. Women can give each other the power to be resilient, which my mother did with me. She suffered a lot but she said, "Nadia will not suffer the same way. Nadia will make change."

Today I volunteer at a refugee camp in Lesbos and I'm going to work for an organization helping migrants and children like me. My dream is to work with the United Nations. I want to become an active agent of peace in my country.

It is still not easy for me. I have been diagnosed with post-traumatic stress. But I am not a victim. After every darkness there is light. And the light is from inside ourselves. We are the light.

BIG BUSH ENERGY
BODY HAIR AS PROTEST

The late 2010s was a time of grown-out armpits and luxuriant pubes as the issue of women's body hair was reclaimed by young feminists as an act of political defiance and feminist celebration.

Women growing out their body hair as an act of feminist rebellion is now more than just acceptable – in the early 2020s, it's hip. In 2018, *Vogue* made a bold statement: "The full bush is the new Brazilian." The trend for women having overly groomed body hair was over, they said, citing some of the hip hairy moments that backed this up: Gaby Hoffman's character on *Girls*, artist Petra Collins who had a peeping bush pic censored by Instagram and Tavi Gevinson saying of a less manicured bush that "it saves time".

Elsewhere there were other signs that razor-ditching was becoming fashionable. By the middle of the decade, the swing towards feminist body hair propagation seemed to have moved beyond more politicized circles and had become a signifier of hipness in the wider context of female beauty. Young women were increasingly using body hair as part of their visual identity, including a clutch of female artists and photographers introducing it into their imagery.

The late 2010s also saw hairy legs and armpits hit advertising: there was the 2017 Adidas Originals image of Swedish photographer and model Arvida Byström (who received death threats when she

Opposite: Photographer Ben Hopper's Natural Beauty project celebrates women who have eschewed depilation. This is a 2019 portrait of musician Camille Alexander.

posted it on her Instagram – itself a quixotic, pink-themed curated space celebrating her body, hair and all). The S/S 2019 campaign for French clothing brand Vetements included a gorgeous model with hairy armpits, and in 2019 actress Emily Ratajkowski wrote an essay in *Harper's Bazaar* saying her pit hair was a feminist expression that made her "feel sexy" (and posed showing it off).

Products aimed at hair-growing millennials sprang up too: new boutique razor brand Billie launched in 2017, with imagery radically showing razors shaving off actual hair in a video directed by photographer Ashley Armitage, who had made her name with female-centric work featuring positive body imagery, often including body hair. Billie also launched a "Project Body Hair" campaign, showing women in swimsuits with luxuriant bikini lines (customers were encouraged to submit their own photos via a hashtag). In 2019, Harry's Razors offshoot Flamingo leaned in to the luxuriance proper when it launched Mons Mist, described as "a conditioning spray for pubic hair and skin that hydrates and nourishes at every stage of growth", along with a "grow choice movement" it called Bush 2020.

It was, of course, during the women's liberation movement of the 1960s and 1970s that the connection between depilation and an oppressive patriarchy first saw women growing out body hair as an expression of feminism. It was a challenging of restrictive beauty standards reflected in the historic boycott of the 1968 Miss America pageant. In *The Female Eunuch* back in 1970, Germaine Greer was railing against the "crude" rationale of depilation for women which rendered them "sexless and infantile"; and in July 1972 the first full issue of *Ms.* magazine ran a cover story editorial entitled: "Body hair: The Last Frontier" with a similar hair-as-feminist-resistance message.

Opposite: The artist Frida Kahlo has been embraced as a body hair icon. In her self-portraits she proudly exaggerated her unibrow and upper lip hair, and was also photographed with bushy armpits.

Right: Julia Roberts made headlines when she revealed her armpit hair for the *Notting Hill* premiere in London, 1999.

Opposite: PJ Harvey spent the 1990s defying perceptions of what a female recording artist should sound like and look like. This image appeared in *NME* in April 1992.

The latest incarnation of hairiness-as-feminism could be seen as part of the trend among Gen Z-ers championing a more "natural" look, alongside plant-based diets and ethical consumption. Makeup brands like Glossier and The Ordinary and fashion labels including Aerie and Reformation went large promoting a dressed-down aesthetic and more diverse, less groomed models during this vogue for "aspirational realness". This coincided with the beginning of a backlash against airbrushing which saw big-name retailers including H&M and CVS leaving their models' arm hair, blemishes and scars on show, picking up the baton started by Dove with their game-changing Real Beauty campaign of 2004.

The latest iteration of the body hair pride movement seems to have risen up alongside feminism in general with millennials embracing the concept of gender fluidity, while those identifying as non-binary and trans women prove that being a "woman" need not be quite so narrowly defined – especially not in terms of hair.

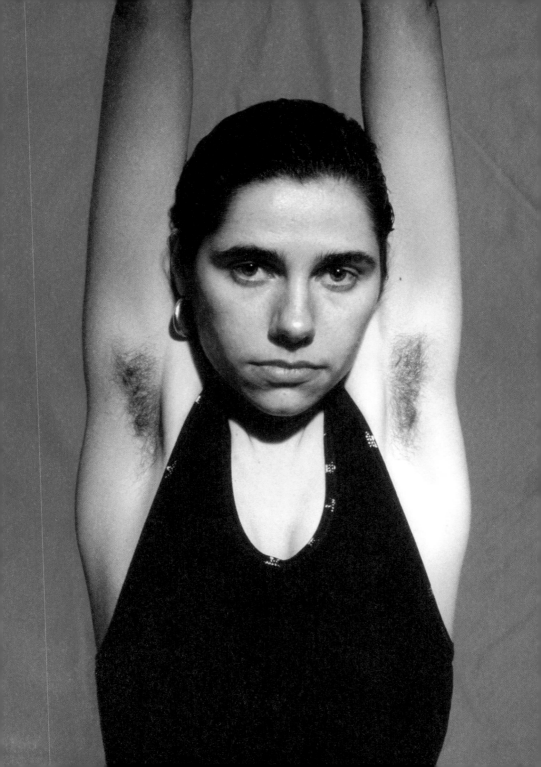

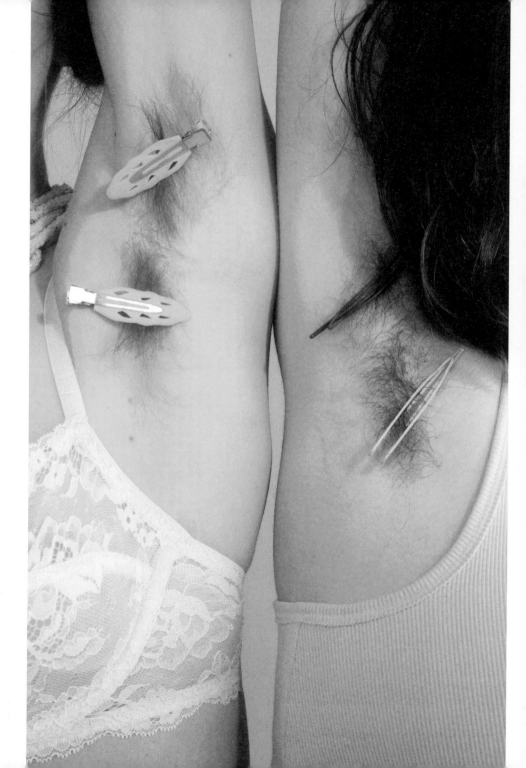

These pages: US photographer Ashley Armitage has made an art of celebrating diverse women with body hair. In 2018 she shot a campaign for new, pro-body hair razor brand Billie — including the first ever commercial to show women removing actual hair.

ALICE COFFIN

JOURNALIST & ACTIVIST

ON BEING PART OF "LA BARBE"

Wearing a beard has been my best feminist move. For the last 10 years, I have been part of one of France's most famous feminist groups: La Barbe (which translates as both "the beard" and "enough!"). The mission of our direct action crew is to invade all-male panels and meetings with fake beards on our faces and congratulate them, ironically, for ensuring the reign of patriarchy.

The group formed in 2007 during the presidential election. For the first time, a woman, Ségolène Royal, was in a position to win, and this generated a flurry of sexist comments from male politicians, even in her own party. She did not win, and so far only men have been president in France. Many cultural, economic, business and sport institutions also remain male-dominated. We go and visit all of them with our beards. I have managed to attend around 150 of our happenings. For this, I have been insulted by MPs, harassed by journalists and mocked by artists. They cannot stand it when we come, as a mirror, to remind them of their sexist supremacy.

Each of our interventions requires strong preparation. The first step is spotting our target and finding a way to infiltrate them. Then, we write a statement we will read on stage which, alongside mocked "congratulations", includes statistics on the number of men invited to speak at the event or selected for their cultural programming. Figures are our best tools. Institutions are always prompt to deny their sexist attitudes – confronting them with numbers helps.

One of our great achievements is fighting the world's most famous movie ceremony: the Cannes Festival. In 2012, we initiated a petition and managed to infiltrate the red carpet to criticize the selection of 22 men out of 22 directors in competition. At the 2020 Césars, 90 per cent of their selected best picture and best director nominees were men. We greeted them with placards saying "More Cleopatras, Less Césars!".

Our group has now spread to other countries such as Mexico, Australia and Denmark, and has received massive media coverage. La Barbe is not only about changing the situation. It is also about empowering ourselves as women. Once you dare to show up on an all-male panel, you have no fear to speak up at a family dinner, in a meeting at your workplace and in everyday life.

CLICKTIVISTS UNITE!

THE HASHTAGS THAT JOINED US

From #MeToo and #TimesUp to #FreetheNipple and #EverydaySexism, modern feminists have used hashtags to link up both off and online, share information and spread messages of protest.

Feminists have always found ways to come together, communicate, express themselves, and disseminate their ideas and messages. The suffragettes had pamphlets, the second wave feminists had consciousness-raising groups, the third wave had magazines, and the fourth wave have the most powerful thing of all: the Internet. Since the 1990s, feminists had begun to gather together online, realizing that the Internet facilitated a more open, globalized form of communication, as well as allowing for the easy spread of information around events such as gigs, marches and meetings. Fanzine culture paved the way for online zines, feminist websites and discussion forums, where like-minded groups, including marginalized subsets of the women's movement such as LGBTQ+ and women of colour, could gather together. The early 2000s saw the widespread take-up of social media networks, beginning with Friendster, MySpace and Facebook, with Twitter and Instagram joining the ranks by 2010.

Social media, in particular, allowed feminists to draw widespread attention to various campaigns, as well as recruit increasingly

Opposite: Originator of #MeToo Tarana Burke with Rose McGowan, 2017.

Right: At the Golden Globes in 2019, Olivia Colman was one of many actors supporting Time's Up.

Opposite: #MeToo emblazoned on a protester's hand during a protest in Paris, 2017.

younger women to the cause. Twitter emerged as the initial dominant platform due to its word-based format and system of hashtagging. Hashtag campaigns blew up post 2010. Early instances included #EverydaySexism, instigated by British writer Laura Bates in 2012 for women to document and call out instances of sexism around the world, followed by Janet Mock's #GirlsLikeUs that sought to bring awareness to the issues affecting trans women. #BlackGirlMagic emerged around 2013 when CaShawn Thompson used it as a way to celebrate and empower women of colour. Beginning around 2014 #FreetheNipple highlighted the double standard when it came to the censure and sexualization of women's bare breasts in general, as well as the banning of the same on social media platforms.

In 2017 hashtag feminism seemed to have reached its zenith when Harvey Weinstein was accused of multiple instances of sexual harassment and assault, and the hashtag #MeToo – created 11 years earlier by activist Tarana Burke – began to be used to demonstrate support and solidarity with his victims. The sheer and staggering number of supporters of the campaign around the world led to a global backlash and calling-out of sexual harassment and assault as well as a lack of female representation in the Hollywood film industry. #TimesUp was launched by the *New York Times* in 2018 with the aim of pushing for pay equality and an end to gender discrimination and sexual harassment "in the workplace and beyond". This included in

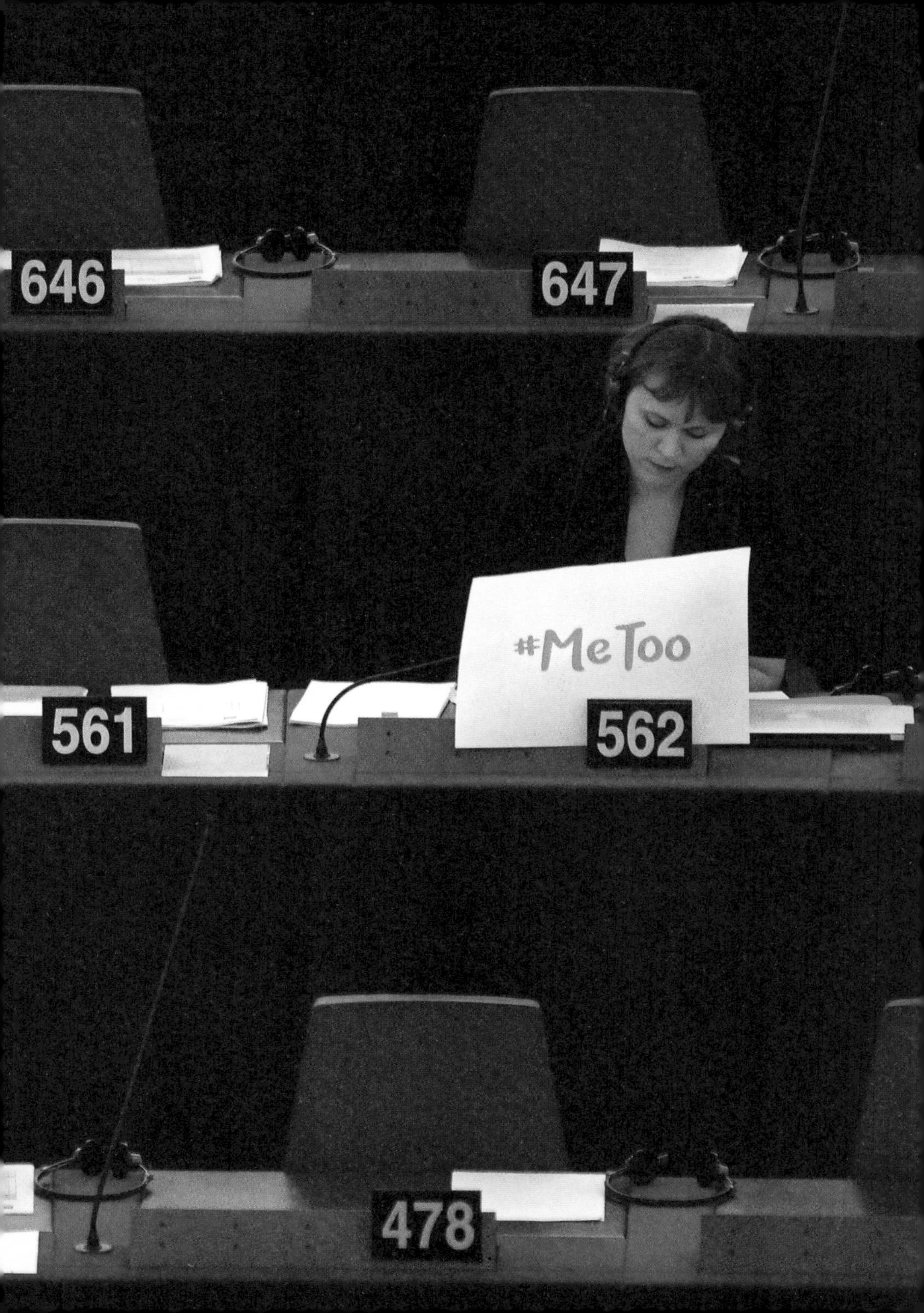
646
647
#MeToo
561
562
478

the film industry, where it had been revealed during the Sony email hacking leak that male stars of the movie *American Hustle* were paid more. The resulting media coverage of the issue put the Hollywood gender pay gap between movie stars at around 56 per cent.

Criticisms of digital feminism activity include discussions around "clicktivism" or "hashtagism", meaning social media activity allows a poster to feel good about themselves, despite the fact that little active protest or real-world change is actually being achieved.

Social media is not a completely open and safe space for feminists. In 2019 it emerged that the Chinese-owned social media app TikTok was actively restricting any pro-LGBTQ+ content in all territories, as well as employing a restrictive, conservative policy in some countries, which banned images of women's cleavage and sanitary protection. The company said after the resulting publicity that it was reconsidering some of the most censorious guidelines. The rise of alt-right bots and trolls has opened conversations about how to protect the feminist digital space, with platforms such as Take Back the Tech and Hackblossom supporting cyber-feminism with information services.

The digital landscape, however, broadly continues to inspire and empower feminists. The recent women's marches proved that social media sharing has the power to effect offline, on-the-ground activism and the sharing of information by women from all countries, backgrounds and races and can be a powerful learning tool and agent of change.

Opposite: In 2017 at the European Parliament during a debate about #MeToo in the EU, Swedish MEP Linnéa Engström sits behind a #MeToo sign. Many MEPs spoke up at the session, demanding a sexual harassment audit of the parliament itself.

FEMINISM GOES POP
HOW BEYONCÉ WAS FLAWLESS

As the messages of the women's movement reached media, the arts, advertising and pop music, artists including Beyoncé began to use their output as a vehicle to spread the word of feminism.

There are few women who have made such an impact on the landscape of modern music and pop culture as the artist known as Beyoncé. She was already a global superstar and icon for black female leadership and empowerment, but in the 2010s Beyoncé's output, including songs, visual imagery and live shows, increasingly seemed to move beyond the palatable pop of "girl power" to more overtly feminist messages. Take, for example, the songs 'Irreplaceable', 'Run the World (Girls)' and 'Pretty Hurts', whose lyrics chart stories of female leadership and impossible, and often racist, Western beauty standards. When she released the song 'Flawless' in 2013, Beyoncé went further, sampling the acclaimed 2012 TED talk given by the Nigerian writer Chimamanda Ngozi Adichie, entitled "We Should All be Feminists" Beyoncé chose to sample Adichie's speech at length, selecting the section about the importance of encouraging female ambition beyond marriage, sex positivity for young women, and sisterhood. Further cementing her emerging identity as an artist who was not afraid to be political, Beyoncé went on to clarify her position, giving a rare interview to *Elle* magazine in which she affirmed her

Opposite: Beyoncé headlined Coachella in 2018, becoming the first black woman to do so. The groundbreaking performance — a celebration of black culture — has been called "historic" and "radical".

belief in equality for women and her identity as a feminist.

On her consequent world tour in 2013–14, titled perhaps pointedly and ironically Mrs Carter, Beyoncé underlined her message by performing in front of giant illuminated letters spelling out the word "FEMINIST", a stage set she also unveiled to millions of viewers of the 2014 MTV Video Music Awards. For an artist who had emerged as someone who wanted to explore themes of female identity, blackness, beauty standards, motherhood and relationships, it was a logical though exciting next step – and a refreshing statement in a media landscape where, despite the pervading coolness of being politicized, young stars can be reluctant to choose sides or alienate potential record buyers, especially in the more politically conservative and religious market of the USA.

Lemonade, the 2016 visual album–slash–film–slash–piece of experimental audio-visual art, saw Beyoncé making the personal political. She employed black female directors including Julie Dash and Kasi Lemmons (as well as taking on the directing mantle herself) to create powerful

Left: In 2016, Beyoncé and her husband Jay-Z showed their support for Democratic presidential nominee (and lifelong feminist) Hillary Clinton.

12 AMAZING FEMINIST POPSTARS

Peaches

A queer, feminist pop icon since her electroclash days in the early 2000s, Canadian-born, Berlin-based Merrill Nisker aka Peaches is now a multidisciplinary artist who plays with gender identity and sex-positivity to thrilling effect.

Lizzo

With her banging anthems, strong LGBTQ+ following, epic music video output and body-positive approach, it was no wonder Lizzo went global in 2019 as the feminist icon who embodies ultra-confidence, self-reliance and self-love.

Rosalía

Spain's powerhouse pop icon has become known for her flamenco-meets-R&B sound, as well as her feminist-themed concept album *El Mal Querer* (The Bad Desire), meaning Rosalía has become an icon of modern Spanish female empowerment.

Anohni

The multimedia-artist formerly known as the music outfit Antony and the Johnsons developed her Future Feminism project in 2014, an exhibition–slash–cultural platform that seeks to redefine and extend feminism in society.

FKA Twigs

Redefining expressions of powerful female sexuality and identity for the 2020s with her contemporary dance, reclaiming of pole-work performance and conceptual videos, Twigs is the art-popstar for the fourth-wave generation.

Lorde

An advocate of intersectional feminism on social media as well as a musical artist who sings about empowerment and identity, Lorde also wore an excerpt from artist Jenny Holzer's *Inflammatory Essays* to the 2018 Grammys, stitched to the back of her gown.

Christine and the Queens

France's Héloïse Letissier puts feminism at the centre of her artistic output, from the political perspectives of her songs and non gender-conforming image to her status as an iconic pansexual queer woman.

M.I.A.

Since her debut in 2003, the British-Sri Lankan rapper Maya Arulpragasam has made musical art out of defiance. Outspoken and unabashedly political, M.I.A has used her platform to start conversations about intersectionality and the limitations of mainstream feminism.

Taylor Swift

2019 saw Swift out herself as a fully fledged feminist with her public stand against sexual assault, further cemented by the release of her album *Lover*, in which she takes lyrical swings at the sexism of the media and music industries.

Grimes

Canada's queen of nerds not only makes, produces and engineers her own weird soundscapes, she has railed against being sexualized, mansplaining and sexism on her Tumblr as well as speaking out on issues such as violence against indigenous Canadian women.

Japanese Breakfast

Alongside her critically acclaimed music career, Michelle Zauner has also written a dazzling memoir examining race, culture and womanhood in a nuanced exploration of intersectionality today.

GIRLI

With music exploring queerness, feminism and mental health, GIRLI has been involved with woman-only arts collective GRL PWR, her concerts have been in partnership with Girls Against, and she is known for throwing tampons into the crowd at gigs.

and beautiful imagery of black women, and a multifaceted narrative that told stories of heartbreak, female empowerment, redemption and forgiveness. 'Formation', especially, emerged as an anthem that was powerful and meaningful for black women in its celebration of pride in your background, identity and power, with an accompanying music video which underlined the message. *Lemonade* was a music-industry game-changer that *Billboard* called "a revolutionary work of black feminism".

Media outlet hot-takes and academics alike have been dissecting Beyoncé's feminist credentials ever since. It is clear that, whatever her exact personal politics, Beyoncé's existence and output has put feminism – and black feminism, in particular – in the global spotlight. In a world where one ill-advised comment made on Twitter can literally ruin a career, that has to count for something. In a music industry still awash with anodyne pop music made only to market to teens, Beyoncé's political powerhouse pop is a refreshing sign of brighter and better things to come.

Opposite: Beyoncé performed at the 2017 Grammys while pregnant with her twins. The all-woman show paid tribute to women and motherhood.

Overleaf: The 2014 MTV VMAs saw Beyoncé performing her empowerment anthem 'Flawless' in front of giant lit-up letters that proclaimed her politics.

HA, HA, HA – BONK
THE AGE OF THE FEMINIST COMEDIANS

Using humour and satire to critique stereotypes, highlight inequality and explore the modern female experience, the 2010s truly belonged to its raft of brilliant funny women.

Amy Schumer. Phoebe Waller-Bridge. Mindy Kaling. Tiffany Haddish. Kate McKinnon. Hannah Gadsby. Katherine Ryan. Leslie Jones. These women made the 2010s the decade in which women were finally allowed to be funny – and went beyond having successful stand-up tours and making manifold TV appearances to become true power-players with the influence to shape the conversation. Never has there been such an important time for women's comedy – some have called it the golden age. Whereas past generations of funny women fought misogyny to claw their way onto late-night TV and panel shows in the 1990s, the 2010s saw women who went much, much further. These women demanded, and took up, space. Who knew they had the skills and intelligence to create their own sitcoms and TV series, which they also wrote, starred in and directed, because they were good at it and they were confident they could. These were women who weren't afraid to centre their stories around women and explore overtly feminist themes.

In the 2010s, women went far beyond sketch shows. The very nature of TV consumption itself helped – the age of streaming is

Opposite: Phoebe Waller-Bridge's hilarious, transgressive *Fleabag* made her name as the voice of millennial women.

allowing women who might otherwise have flown under the radar to take their shows to a wider, global audience. (Some comedians such as Tiffany Haddish paid this forward; she dedicated her 2019 special, *Tiffany Haddish Presents: They Ready*, to shining a spotlight on her favourite underexposed female comedians.) In 2004 Mindy Kaling began the wave, when she was hired as a writer–performer on the American version of *The Office*, the only woman on the team. *The Mindy Project*, which Kaling wrote, produced and starred in, allowed her to create a female-led staff, while 2019 film *Late Night* cemented her presence as a bankable Hollywood talent.

Amy Schumer began to break records from 2016, when she appeared on Forbes' annual "World's Highest-paid Comedians" list. It had previously been all male since its inception in 2006, with the exception of one appearance by Chelsea Handler. Today, Schumer has carved out a multifaceted career for herself, which began when she made art of feminist-slanted satire through her topical and hilarious Comedy Central show *Inside Amy Schumer*. Her sketches explored rape culture and body image, and included "Last Fuckable Day", exploring Hollywood's pervasive ageism and sexism, and the award-winning meta parody "Twelve Angry Men", in which men debated whether Schumer was "hot enough" to be on television. Next came writing and starring in *Trainwreck*, a film which grappled with slut-shaming and workplace discrimination, followed by several other Hollywood roles, two Netflix specials (one she did while pregnant, about being pregnant) and a multi-million-dollar Spotify podcast deal. Overtly political, Schumer uses Instagram to advocate for parental leave, voter registration, gun control and Planned Parenthood. She was also the first female stand-up to headline Madison Square Garden (she opened for Madonna in 2016).

Phoebe Waller-Bridge's *Fleabag* – derived from her 2013 one-

Opposite: *The Mindy Project* pilot aired in 2012 making Mindy Kaling the first woman of colour to create, write and star in a primetime sitcom.

woman Edinburgh Fringe Festival show and reinvented as a BBC comedy–drama – was career changing for the writer-performer. This was thanks not only to meme-able sequences such as #HotPriest and #Obamawank, but to the writer's portrayal of the eponymous female protagonist in all her complicated, flawed and funny glory. Fleabag argues with her sister and gets into crap relationships, defining the particular ennui of the modern millennial woman. Waller-Bridge's subsequent development deal with Amazon and a sweep of awards – along with other successful female-centric projects such as the quirky buddy comedy–slash–spy thriller that is *Killing Eve* – proved that women around the world were hungry for on-screen stories that showed multi-dimensional women and made them laugh. After all, they needed it.

Above: Amy Schumer's sketch "Milk, Milk, Lemonade" parodied music industry hyper-sexualization, as well as "booty anthems".

Opposite: Comedian and actor Tiffany Haddish in 2018, the same year she used a Netflix special to highlight other female comedians.

THE F WORD
THE RISE OF FEMINIST PUBLISHING

The late 2010s saw an unprecedented demand for feminist books, with bestsellers in the form of essay collections and manifestos, histories and speculative fantasies. Welcome to the bright new age of feminist publishing.

When Beyoncé released her song 'Flawless' in 2013, it was credited as "FT Chimamanda Ngozi Adichie". The song felt like a declaration of feminist intent with its passionate lyrics about notions of female beauty. In it, Beyoncé chose to sample audio – at length – from a TED Talk that became a book-length essay, very simply entitled "We Should All Be Feminists", by award-winning Nigerian novelist Adichie. That book would go on to become a bestseller and Adichie an internationally celebrated figurehead for modern global feminism. In 2017, Dior put "We Should All Be Feminists" on a $710 T-shirt and sent it down the catwalk.

There are other moments that have signalled we are experiencing a seminal moment for feminist texts in culture. First there was Caitlin Moran's 2011 memoir-slash-manual *How to be a Woman*, which advocated leopard-print wearing and pubic-hair growing and became a huge bestseller in multiple countries. The same year, Laura Bates's *Everyday Sexism* project – already a sensation on the Internet

Opposite: Covers of books that have recently made waves in the publishing industry around the world. *Good Night Stories for Rebel Girls* has been a global sensation, and Margaret Atwood's classic *The Handmaid's Tale* re-entered the bestseller list nearly 30 years after its original publication.

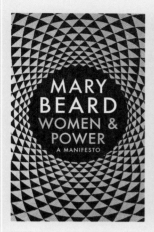

Bad
———
Feminist
———
Essays

Roxane
———
Gay

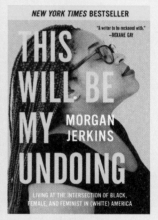

Men
Explain
Things
to Me

REBECCA SOLNIT
author of *A Paradise Built in Hell*

and on social media – became a bestseller when it transitioned to print. A raft of feminist-slanted non-fiction appeared in its wake, making bestsellers of essay collections (repeat that to yourself, and dance: Bestselling. Feminist. Essay collections) such as Roxane Gay's *Bad Feminist* and Rebecca Solnit's *Men Explain Things to Me*, both published to great acclaim in 2014. Other writers of feminist memoirs came forward to give first-hand accounts of the twenty-first-century female experience – such as Jessica Valenti's *Sex Object*, which became a *New York Times* bestseller when it was published in 2016.

The spotlight, too, turned on feminist reappraisal of the past with classicist and committed feminist Mary Beard's *Women & Power: A Manifesto* – a massive bestseller in numerous countries which has already been described as a "A modern feminist classic" (*Guardian*). Meanwhile, a slew of novels focusing on female stories and feminist retellings of myths and legends appeared on prize lists, such as Naomi Alderman's dystopian feminist fantasy *The Power* and Madeline Miller's *Circe*. The political climate no doubt has encouraged this female-focused printed uprising: when Trump was elected in 2016, Margaret Atwood's 1985 novel *The Handmaid's Tale* re-entered the bestseller list, spending 88 weeks there and selling more than three million copies, while the handmaid's costume of red robe and white bonnet, as seen in the TV adaptation of the novel, has become an international symbol of protest against patriarchal oppression. (Atwood's Gilead-based sequel, *The Testaments*, was published in September 2019 and became an instant bestseller, co-winning the Man Booker Prize with Bernardine Evaristo's *Girl, Woman, Other*.)

This feminist publishing phenomenon hasn't just extended to the realm of adult literature – in 2016 two Italian women, Elena Favilli and Francesca Cavallo, decided children's literature was severely lacking when it came to stories of inspirational women of the past, and ran a Kickstarter campaign to publish their illustrated compendium of women's histories, *Good Night Stories for Rebel Girls*. It caused a publishing sensation – not only did *Rebel Girls* break all records when it became the most-funded original book in the history of crowdfunding, raising $1.3 million from backers across 75 countries – it has gone on to become a huge global bestseller, inspiring numerous similar children's titles and series and permanently changing the landscape of children's books.

This historic wave of feminist publishing looks set to continue, with prize lists increasingly becoming populated by women's stories and voices, and publishers continuing to invest heavily in feminist books (including this one) into the next decade. It's proof that feminism truly has entered the mainstream and has taken up residence in the collective consciousness. The proof is in the print.

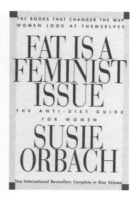

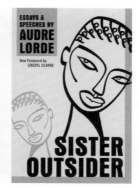

Left: Iconic feminist books of the twentieth century explored the ideas of the second wave from gender roles and beauty standards to race, class and sexuality.

FEMINIST READING LIST

A Vindication of the Rights of Woman (1792)
Mary Wollstonecraft

This radical work of proto-feminist philosophy argues that women should enjoy the rights and civil liberties that men assumed automatically, as well as education.

The Awakening (1899)
Kate Chopin

The story of a depressed wife and mother who is emboldened by a passionate affair to escape her mediocre existence for a life of creative freedom is considered an important work of early feminist fiction.

Herland (1915)
Charlotte Perkins Gilman

Based on a utopia about an isolated civilization of only women, Herland critiques the stifling oppression that the economic subjugation of women creates and dares to imagine a society without it.

A Room of One's Own (1929)
Virginia Woolf

Based on lectures delivered by Woolf in 1928, this proto-feminist essay explores the history of women's literary achievements, arguing for women's education and the enablement of women's creativity.

The Second Sex (1949)
Simone de Beauvoir

This study of what it means to be a woman and analysis of history from a female perspective is groundbreaking in its viewpoint of the inequality and otherness embodied by womanhood.

The Golden Notebook (1962)
Doris Lessing

Telling the story of the breakdown of a writer, mother and political activist, this famous experimental novel is also about a woman's search for identity in the challenging climate of 1950s Britain.

The Bell Jar (1963)
Sylvia Plath

Suffering from an intense depression, but also on a quest to discover her identity as a woman, the story of Esther Greenwood is a fictionalized account of Plath's own life and struggles with mental health.

Wide Sargasso Sea (1966)
Jean Rhys

This modern classic is both a prequel and critical response to Jane Eyre, giving voice and substance to the original "madwoman in the attic", taking in colonialism, slavery, racism and Victorian sexuality.

I Know Why the Caged Bird Sings (1969)
Maya Angelou

Angelou's first volume of memoir traces her own difficult beginnings in the 1930s South as well as exploring issues at the heart of American history – segregation, racism and sexual abuse.

The Female Eunuch (1970)
Germaine Greer

Offering a broad examination of the various manifestations of sexism and patriarchal repression, Greer takes on body image, sexuality, beauty, constructs of femininity and female identity in sassy, exuberant style.

Sexual Politics (1970)
Kate Millett

This pioneering academic work is one of the first pieces of feminist criticism to become a bestseller, making its author an enduring icon of the early women's liberation movement.

The Bluest Eye (1970)
Toni Morrison

Exploring internalized racism as well as female shame and trauma, Morrison's important debut novel is a profound and heartbreaking story which centres on the unloved and abused Pecola Breedlove who believes that blue eyes are the answer to all her troubles.

Of Woman Born: Motherhood as Experience and Institution (1976)
Adrienne Rich
Investigating the state of motherhood from a feminist perspective, this is the feminist poet's adventure into scholarly analysis, incorporating journal extracts, historical account and reflections.

The Women's Room (1977)
Marilyn French
The story of a conventional housewife and mother in 1950s America, and her gradual feminist awakening, *The Women's Room* is considered to be a landmark feminist novel of the twentieth century.

Fat is a Feminist Issue (1978)
Susie Orbach
Taking in past trauma, self-worth, negative body image, compulsive eating and notions of female self-sacrifice, this 1970s bestseller is an empowering manual advocating for self-love and acceptance.

Women, Race and Class (1981)
Angela Davis
Recounting the history of slavery and civil rights along with suffragism, Davis critiques the racism and class privilege embodied in second wave feminism and highlights icons of black women's empowerment.

Ain't I a Woman: Black Women and Feminism (1981)
bell hooks
A study of how black women have been historically oppressed, *Ain't I a Woman* addresses the limitations of white second wave feminism and argues for a new kind of intersectionality.

Right-Wing Women (1983)
Andrea Dworkin
This critique of capitalism and the Right is just as provocative and radical as it was on publication as it touches on the oppressive power of domestic abuse, restricted abortions and some forms of religion.

Sister Outsider (1984)
Audre Lorde

The collected writings of the radical, black, lesbian poet include beautiful, sometimes lyrical, reflections on racism, sexism, ageism, friendship, sexuality and homophobia.

The Handmaid's Tale (1985)
Margaret Atwood

This sinister speculative tale of a patriarchal society of subjugated women resurfaced when the red handmaid costumes worn in the TV adaptation became a powerful symbol of anti-Trump resistance.

The Beauty Myth (1990)
Naomi Wolf

Taking on the societal beauty standards impressed on women as seen in advertising, magazines, the fashion industry and more, Wolf argues that repressive notions of beauty are a harmful patriarchal force.

Backlash (1991)
Susan Faludi

This bestseller introduced the American public to the anti-feminist backlash of the 90s and explores continuing attacks on women's rights, including the glass ceiling, reproductive rights and workplace sexism.

Persepolis (2000)
Marjane Satrapi

An autobiographical account of the author's early life in 1980s Iran, this graphic novel is a funny, moving and eye-opening exploration of the impact of war and religious extremism on women.

Hood Feminism (2021)
Mikki Kendall

A rigorous examination of sexual orientation, class, race, disability and gender, Hood Feminism is an all-encompassing look at feminism and its history, centring the BIPOC voices that have been pushed to the side for too long.

DIANA EVANS

NOVELIST & AUTHOR
OF *ORDINARY PEOPLE*

ON OWNING FEMINISM

Feminism is inside. It is not something we adopt, or can pretend to be, or partially be. It is of the blood and spirit, engendered early, in our formation, as belief, a way of feeling and existing and thinking in the world. For me, it was born in a childhood cage of domestic patriarchy, in which the father ruled and the women were apparently ruled. Inside, though, I was never ruled. I was strong and electric and aware of the depth of my own power. I understood that this microcosm in which I existed was imbalanced and would be defiantly corrected in the course of my future life outside it. Or perhaps it is more that I developed this defiance once arriving on the outside.

There are forms of outward or surface feminism that I do not trust: pretty feminism, pop feminism, girl power. That shouty brandishing of the feminist label while performing for the approval of the conventional, voyeuristic male gaze. It is a pretence, a lie. It sends a dangerous and disempowering message that your agency is abundant only in the capsule of your compliance, your hardworking (diets, weaves, skin lighteners, make-up) adherence to the aesthetic of mainstream beauty, which has harangued and oppressed women for so long. This is not to say that we should not be beautiful, or treasure our beauty, but that there is deeper power in recognizing how it has been used against us, as a form of control, as an associate to abuse, perpetually undervaluing the power of the self that lies beneath, where the real power lies.

Calling myself feminist is like calling my own name. I am a witness to the movement as well as a beneficiary of it. I lie quietly in its valley, yet it simultaneously lies within me, with its own particular face and nature and its own particular voice.

BLACK GIRL MAGIC
RALLY CRY, CELEBRATION, EMPOWERMENT

The story of how one woman's simple social media hashtag grew to become a huge worldwide online movement celebrating black women, their power, identity and achievements.

In 2016, as part of a video series by *Essence* and *Time*, the then President Barack Obama and Misty Copeland, principal dancer of the American Ballet Theatre, sat down to explore the pertinent issues of the day for twenty-first-century women and girls. On the table for discussion was the impact of modern social activism and the digital sphere as an agent of change, and the importance of positive representation on social media for women of colour, including a hashtag that had, in the years preceding the interview, become a life-affirming symbol of pride and empowerment for millions of black women around the world – the hashtag #BlackGirlMagic.

"I think it couldn't be more positive for a young black girl to see that it's okay to be yourself," Copeland said. "It's okay to not have to transform and look like what you may see on the cover of a lot of magazines. That you are beautiful, that it's possible to succeed in any field that you want to, looking the way that you do. With your hair the way it is."

Though it had circulated on the Internet for some time, #BlackGirlMagic is generally accepted to have been popularized by

Opposite: A piece from the 2020 Black Girl Magic series of artworks by artist Marina Esmeraldo and DJ and activist Honey Dijon.

Above: *Essence* magazine's Black Girl Magic Class of 2016 issue celebrated talented young black women.

Opposite: Michelle Obama speaks onstage at Black Girls Rock! in Newark, New Jersey, 2015.

activist CaShawn Thompson in about 2013, as a movement-defining statement. Thompson later told the *L.A. Times*, "I say 'magic' because it's something that people don't always understand. Sometimes our accomplishments might seem to come out of thin air because a lot of times, the only people supporting us are other black women."

#BlackGirlMagic swiftly gained traction, both as a social media device and as a concept, catching fire as conversations about diversity, representation and equality intensified in the wake of 2012's #BlackLivesMatter. The increased discussions around the necessity for a truly intersectional feminism went mainstream, and

the enthusiasm with which #BlackGirlMagic was caught up and used made it clear that women of colour needed a space to own that lifted them up and celebrated their achievements. The Obama presidency – and Michelle Obama's resulting activism focusing on women and girls – seemed to give the movement even more momentum, opening up the conversation around the black female experience in the highest corridors of power. In 2015 the First Lady gave a speech at the Black Girls Rock! awards, speaking of the pressure on black girls not to step up to lead and to look a certain way. The following year *Essence*'s February 2016 edition was emblazoned with the cover line "Black Girl Magic Class of 2016", highlighting a feature which profiled high-achieving, inspirational women of colour.

#BlackGirlMagic has since been referenced in countless editorials and newspaper reports; it was mentioned in a song by Janelle Monáe; it was unpacked in a discussion between Solange Knowles and academic and commentator Melissa Harris-Perry; op-eds around the world discussed whether the hashtag was uplifting or limiting (by potentially taking focus away from the real problems faced by many women of colour the world over).

At the time of writing, #BlackGirlMagic has 30.9 million posts on Instagram, tagging everything from images of smiling best friends, family portraits and graduations, to celebrities, beauty shots and mirror selfies. There are women in scrubs and women lifting weights, women in bridesmaids' dresses and women holding babies. Women brought together to celebrate themselves.

Opposite: In 2018 Instagram threw a celebration for #BlackGirlMagic and #BlackCreatives in NYC. These models have braided hairstyles designed by Susy Oludele.

Overleaf: In 2018 these 19 African American women ran for judgeships in Harris County, Texas using the slogan "Black Girl Magic" for their campaign – and, historically, all of them were elected.

CONCLUSION

This book bears witness to the incredible achievements of the women's movement: 120 years of feminists battling for equality, with the last 50 seeing seismic shifts effected through campaigning, activism and resistance.

In the twenty-first century, feminism has truly gone mainstream. Women all over the world are openly, actively feminist. The Internet and social media are powerful tools through which women share experiences and ideas, form uplifting communities and find information. Technological advancements including the pill, new abortion legislation, quota schemes and the rise of flexible at-home virtual working have all enabled a slightly more level playing field for working women – though, it should be noted that The Fawcett Societ's Equal Pay Day report showed the damaging effect the global pandemic had on equality in the workplace, estimating that over a third (35 per cent) of working mothers had lost work or hours due to childcare demands. Still, we are now more likely to work in STEM subjects and appear more frequently in boardrooms – though the share of female *Fortune* 500 CEOs has slumped since its 2017 high of 6.4 per cent. In 2021 NASDAQ announced that they were introducing a policy that required publicly trading companies to have at least one woman on their board of directors. The move came after a review that found around 75 per cent of companies did not meet the threshold. Some developed countries have instituted positive discrimination systems to ensure gender parity in politics, and women have high-profile roles in governance, campaign as White House candidates and lead countries.

When the Tokyo 2020 Olympics (delayed for a year due to Covid-19) kicked off in 2021, it was the most gender-balanced Games in history, with women representing almost 49 per cent of participating athletes.

A wave of female TV and film creators has been rising up to give voice to the female experience since the late 2010s, such as Michaela Coel, Sharon Horgan, Lisa McGee and Aisling Bea. At the 2021 Oscars, Chloé Zhao made history when she became the first woman of colour and the first woman of Asian descent to earn best director at the Academy Awards. She remains only the second woman to win the award.

Because of this, a huge tonal shift has occurred in popular culture, with feminist messages now seen in books, music, film, TV, art and advertising. Depictions of women increasingly reflect a more diverse, body-positive reality. The growing acceptance of gender as non-binary is creating greater freedom for those excluded by patriarchal stereotypes. There are conversations in the media about rape culture, diversity, trans acceptance, #EverydaySexism, stereotyping and period pride. Protests all over the world speaking truth to power are now frequent occurrences. Women are being educated to demand better, ask for pay rises, break down barriers and take up more space.

There is still much to be done, especially in the developing world where women and girls have restricted access to education and opportunities, endure FGM and forced marriage, and live below the poverty line. In August 2021, Kabul fell to the Taliban. Afghan women are now unable to work and girls are banned from attending secondary school. Despite the danger, Afghan women have been taking to the streets in protest, and speaking out, against the oppressive regime.

In Britain, a 2020 Fawcett Society study found that pay parity for British women was "decades away" and that we remain extremely underrepresented across politics, public life and business. Women of colour, LGBTQ+ women and differently abled women still face daily discriminatory barriers making them even less likely to be represented.

For now, we can look back at over 100 years of the women's movement and know that we will do what we have always done. We'll keep fighting.

Overleaf: Female Democratic lawmakers during President Trump's 2019 State of the Union Address. They wore white as a tribute to the suffragettes and in solidarity with women.

INDEX

CREDITS